Coming Together

Portrait of a Family

By

Winona Garmhausen

ISBN: 1-4140-4400-3 (e-book)
ISBN: 1-4140-4401-1 (Paperback)

Library of Congress Control Number: 2003099399

This book is printed on acid free paper.

Printed in the United States of America
Bloomington, IN

Cover photo
> Frederick Kunz and Viola Lause photo
> taken 1926 at the Lause homestead.

1stBooks – rev. 02/09/04

Dedicated to all the women of our ancestry, of whom so little has been recorded but to whom most sincere thanks are extended, for their strength, courage and perseverance in making homes for us all in the new West.

An Acknowledgement

I have pondered over the last two decades how I would, when the time finally came, thank everyone who had helped me along the way. I must truly say that my work was accomplished through "the kindness of strangers." How can one possibly thank the hundreds of kind people who over the years at libraries and historical societies never hesitated to respond to my queries? How would one thank all the friends that were made as the road was traveled and common interests found? I often remarked on this journey that one caught up in genealogical research should either be retired or rich, or both. To which many folks who were bent over their microfilms machines or peering through magnifying glasses readily, and sometimes a bit ironically, agreed. But since I was neither, the phone, the fax, e-mail, and the amazingly dependable United States Post Office became my best tools of discovery. The Internet, which many have found to be such an invaluable tool, was of little help to me as very little has been recorded that could provide even the smallest clue to our lineage. Only once did I employ a professional researcher and that was a most rewarding experience. When it comes to translating old German handwriting nothing can substitute for a multilingual German professional. It is my opinion that the genealogy community, amateur or professional, can be held up as a shining example of people who care about people and never hesitate to lend a hand when and where needed. For that I give my most heartfelt thanks and hope this volume will in some way be a thank-you gift to all who so graciously helped me on my twenty-year journey.

My deepest thanks go to Ronald and Carol Kunz whose two decades of effort can be seen in the photographs found throughout this volume and in the Pedigree Chart which ends it.

Table of Contents

List of Illustrations

Preface

The intent of this narrative is to show how it was that our parents, Frederick Kunz and Viola Lause, came together by way of generations of immigrant settlers to northwest Ohio. It is not an attempt to lay a complete historical framework over each time period from 1790 when some of our first ancestors came to the Ohio country. There are scores of books and articles that cover these events in great factual detail. Rather, it is an attempt, based on more than twenty years of genealogical research, to introduce our parents' ancestors in the framework of the times in an easy to comprehend manner. So that the narrative may flow more smoothly, a pedigree chart which contains the vital statistics of each ancestor as well as biographical material in so far as it is known as of this printing is included with this volume.

It is my sincere hope that this volume can be a starting point for many who are attempting to find relatives in our ancestral line. And, perhaps, for others offer an additional fact or two that would fill in missing areas of their research. Genealogical material will be found up to and including the date of our parents' wedding in November of 1929. No information is provided beyond that point out of respect for the privacy of our mother, now 94, and our siblings. It should be noted, however, that various family members have contributed genealogical material to the Delphos Ohio Public Library which is available to the public for research at the library. Especially helpful are the volumes contributed by Ronald and Carol Kunz of Delphos, Ohio. The Kunzes have recorded, in addition to their families' genealogies, the records of St. John's Catholic Church, local funeral homes, and area cemeteries.

For my part, since I was not yet born when their Pedigree Chart ends, I have endeavored to show something of the personalities of our parents from my childhood memories and family stories. To not do so would reduce our parents to the cardboard cutouts of posed pictures. To further avoid this stereotype, the photos I have chosen of them show a young couple having fun and enjoying their late teens and early twenties. These were, after all, the "Roaring Twenties" when one was expected to be carefree and gay.

Immediately following the illustrated text are a list of suggested readings, and content notes end each chapter of the book, as needed. The purpose of each is to give the reader further assistance in tracing a relative of whom mention was made. It is hoped that these tools will make the researcher's task a bit easier than was mine and spare him or her the tedium and expense of prolonged genealogical research.

What follows is considered a work in progress and open to change, addition, and correction. I would greatly appreciate hearing from family members and others who have had the good fortune to uncover additional information on our ancestors. It is also my hope that in the not-too-distant-future a young cousin, niece, nephew, or grandchild will pick up this story and carry it on through the succeeding generations. This manuscript is just a beginning.

Winona Garmhausen
Bloomington, Indiana
October 30, 2003

Introduction

In 1994, having lived in Santa Fe, New Mexico for more than 22 years and having become thoroughly steeped in the Native American lore of the area, I was not a bit surprised when I began to find myself coming full circle back to my Midwest beginnings. The Indians of the Southwest believe that life is like a dance, moving in and out but always coming back to connect the circle.

In the spring of 1993 I had begun having a repetitive dream. This dream always centered on the city of Cincinnati, Ohio. The implied message of all these colorful and plotless dreams was that I should travel to Cincinnati and that for some yet unexplained reason I just needed to be there. If I had been involved in the New Age Movement, as many in Santa Fe are, I would have viewed such a happening with great seriousness, but as a transplanted mid-westerner through and through I found that the dreams became something of an uneasy joke to laugh about with family and friends.

To make these dreams even more inexplicable and perplexing was the fact that I came to the Southwest from northern Ohio, and although I had visited Cincinnati many times, nothing in those visits compelled me to move south to that location while an Ohio resident. In fact, all my thoughts and aspirations had pulled me west away from Ohio and Indiana, my joint home states.

Perhaps, I thought, spending so much of my time the previous ten years researching my midwestern ancestors had stimulated these senseless nighttime wanderings.

About this same time many elements of my genealogical research began to come together. As I dug deeper and deeper into my family history in the area surrounding Lima, Ohio, I discovered that my family's history did not include just land-seeking Europeans willing to use any means to attain their goal and totally disregarding the rights of Native Americans, but that I had ancestors who had lived side by side with the Indians of northern Ohio for a good part of our early history.

On a research trip to Ohio in the summer of 1993, I came across an entry in an old Allen County, Ohio, history volume relating to one of my great-great-grandfathers, Edward Hartshorn, and his son,

Elmore. Edward Hartshorn was an attorney and a judge living in Allen County in the early 1830s.

The story was of an incident that took place when the Shawnee Indian Chief Pe-Aitch-Ta (also called PHT) had been accused of stealing by a white neighbor named Billy Lippincott. Chief Pe-Aitch-Ta called Lippincott a liar to his face, saying, "Ah, Billy Lippincott, you be one big lie." Constable Elmore Hartshorn brought Pe-Aitch-Ta to a Justice, most probably his father Edward. The Justice dismissed the case based on PHT's testimony.[1]

Our family's story could not be told, I realized, without making every effort to define the role we had played in the settlement of the Northwest Territory and especially in the northwest corner of Ohio where all our ancestors ultimately chose to settle.

Once the circle begins to close, I soon found out, events in one's life seem to magically fall in place until at some point you are no longer surprised by connections but, indeed, begin to expect them.

When I related the new discovery of my ancestor Hartshorn and the Shawnee Indian Chief to a Pueblo Indian friend, he suggested that I might enjoy reading a book that he had just finished on the life of Tecumseh, the great Shawnee warrior. The book entitled *Panther in the Sky* was written by a well-known Midwest author, James Alexander Thom, who has written numerous fictional but carefully researched accounts of Indian men and women of the eighteenth and nineteenth centuries. Once I began reading Thom's books, I found myself fascinated by his subject matter and writing style, and I set about reading all his books which concern not only the lives of Native American men and women but also the settlement of the near and far west. All in some ways were related to the story that I eventually wanted to tell about my family and their early days in the new western frontier.

The last link in the chain of events came about as serendipitously as the other events and by this time was no longer a surprise but a realization that surely this was all leading somewhere. First the inscrutable dreams followed by the genealogy discoveries, then introduction to the books that addressed the very periods and geographical areas encompassing my family's history. What other link could there be to my homeland that was nudging me further to re-explore my ties to the Midwest?

My research, study, and publishing in the Southwest had centered around the unique Santa Fe institution, The Institute of American Indian Arts (IAIA), and I continued to have many ties to the school long after I had published a book on its history.* I lived in a rural area outside of Santa Fe and rented out a small guesthouse on my property, most often to students or teachers at the Institute. When the guesthouse was vacated in the fall of 1993 and was advertised, I received a call from an instructor at the IAIA about its availability. We agreed upon a date to occupy and in September of that year, Shawnee Indian poet and author Barney Bush moved in just across from my little adobe house to stay until Christmastime. During that time we became friends and discussed our mutual interest and fondness for the IAIA as we shared many stories concerning its hopeful beginnings in 1962 and its troubled present.

We also had long talks about Shawnee history and traditions. At one point in such a conversation I expressed my desire and need to further explore the Midwest in search of my ancestors and their early neighbors, the Shawnee. Barney suggested to me that I might like to visit the United Remnant Band of Shawnees, a group of Shawnees from throughout the country that had begun to reclaim their traditions and lands near Urbana, Ohio. The Ohio Shawnee's Chief since the 1960s has been Hawk Pope, a descendent of Thick Water, who was Tecumseh's friend and fellow warrior. Barney Bush had grown up principally in the southern hills of Illinois, and he and Hawk Pope were friends of long standing. He suggested that I call Hawk Pope to arrange a meeting with the United Remnant Band when I next visited Ohio.

---

* **The Institute of American Indian Arts was established in 1962 by the Bureau of Indian Affairs and is open to college-age students from all American Indian and Alaskan Native Tribes. The focus of its curriculum is an integration of Native American arts and formal academic study leading to careers in many aspects of the arts and museum studies. Please consult my previous work, *History of Indian Arts Education In Santa Fe* (Sunstone Press, 1988) for complete historical background of this unique institution.**

Early in the spring of 1994 I called Hawk Pope as I planned for a May and June research trip throughout the Midwest. He was most gracious and invited me to attend a Bread Dance Ceremony to be held in mid-May at their tribal site called "Shawandasse" near Urbana. I made mention that I was very impressed with Thom's books on the Shawnee, and he commented in return that his tribal members had been Thom's consultants on many aspects of Shawnee life for his writing and later for films made from his books. James Alexander Thom, a non-Indian, and his Shawnee Indian wife Dark Rain had greatly assisted the Tribe in re-establishing themselves in their home location. Chief Pope further informed me that, in appreciation of his support and friendship, Thom had been honored by the Tribe and made an honorary member a few years before. And as an aside he asked if I knew that James Alexander Thom was married to Hawk's own sister.

With that chance remark, the circle closed for me. The past was not just lists of births and marriages and deaths listed on huge charts of paper and filed away on computer disks. The past was very much alive and we were still interconnected. Now was the time to put heart and flesh on these skeletal forms.

Perhaps, I thought, I was not so immune to dreams and portents after all. Hadn't my dreams and Indian friends led me one by one to find that, just as my immigrant ancestors had survived through their descendants, so had the Native Americans of the Ohio country survived against great and terrible odds to re-inhabit the land that was once so cruelly wrested from them by the very relatives whose memories I had held dear? Clearly, this was a journey of discovery that must be taken.

And where to start? Why, Cincinnati, of course. One must start somewhere and what better place to start than where dreams take you. It was my belief that this is how my ancestors had begun their quest, and armed with a little of their courage and a great deal of optimism, I began a journey over the next five years which would teach me a sympathy for and understanding of those admirable (and some not so admirable) pioneers of the Midwest.

Notes

[1] The story of Indian Chief PHT and his adversary Billy Lippincott can be found in the *History of Allen County*. It is reasonable to assume that the "Justice" in this case was Edward Hartshorn, who is mentioned repeatedly in Allen County histories during this time period, most frequently for his performance of wedding ceremonies.

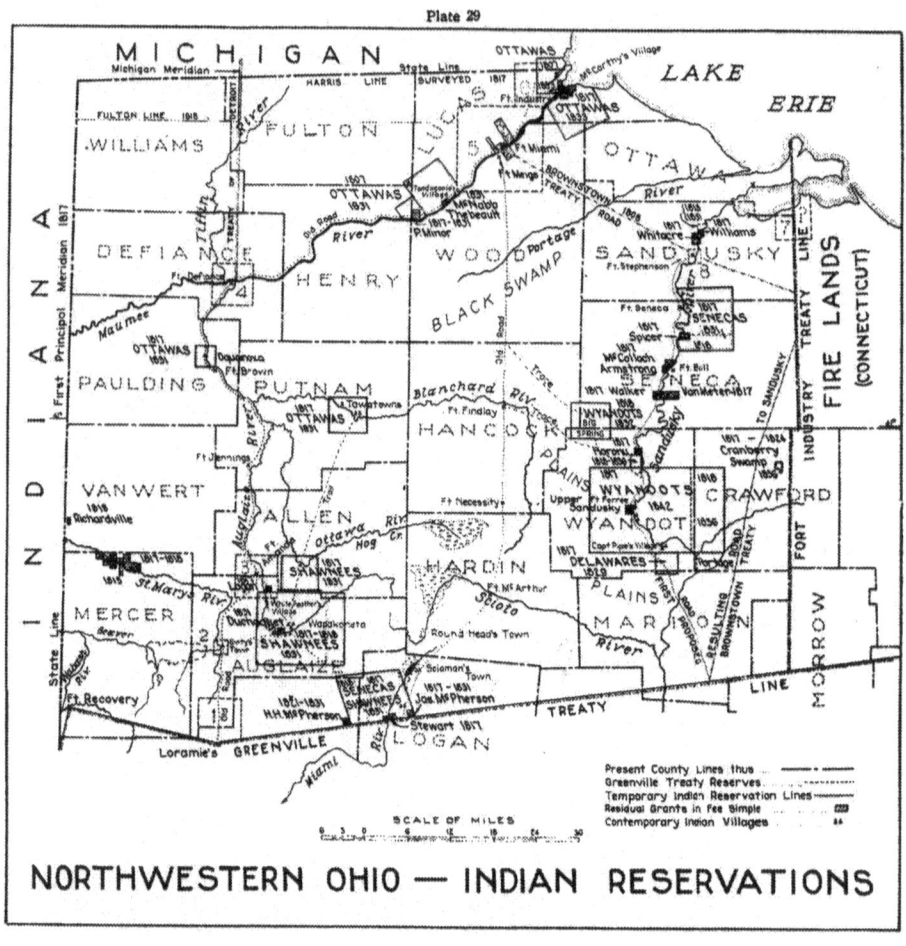

Map courtesy of Ohio State Auditor, Columbus, Ohio.

Chapter One: 1790, The Arrival

Sitting on the bank of the Ohio River on the Kentucky side in the summer of 1994, I made a remarkable discovery. It was not the city that I had come here to re-discover, but the magnificent Ohio River. The city of Cincinnati sits directly across from the community of Covington, Kentucky, and in between is the wide and beautiful expanse of this historical waterway. I was certain this was my reason for being so preoccupied with the "dream" of returning to Cincinnati. This river was the lifeline for many who traveled to the newly defined Northwest Territory in the late eighteenth and early nineteenth centuries. Thousands of persons from the eastern territories and states set out for the many ports along the Ohio at great risk to their lives. Beset by dangers of the river itself as well as conflicts on both sides of the river, they traveled by flatboat, keelboat, or canoe with their families, friends, animals, and possessions to disembark at Cincinnati and Fort Washington. From this point many settlers of the Northwest Territory would in time travel northward to inhabit central and northern Ohio, and many others would move farther north and west to pioneer Indiana, Michigan, and the other states formed from the Northwest Territory.

Over the next few years I traveled the banks of that marvelous and powerful river many times, and it became a living symbol to me of the lives of the native and non-native inhabitants of the Ohio River country. I have dipped little bottles into its seemingly muddy waters at Cincinnati, Marietta, and many small stops in between. The contents of these little containers are as sacred to me as must be the waters of the Ganges and the Nile to the inhabitants of those far away places. I keep them about my little home and studio as reminders of what this grand and abundant river has meant to the pasts of millions of Americans. In the early centuries of our new Republic, the rivers meant travel, opportunity, commerce, growth, change, and prosperity. To the early immigrant, the Ohio was the also the pathway to the Mississippi and the farthermost reaches of what was then considered the Far West.

It was down this river that my paternal grandmother's family, the Clawsons, came in 1789 or 1790.[1] These were dangerous times and

1

settlers to the Ohio country were well aware of the difficulties ahead when they gathered to make plans to pull up stakes and set out once more to the new western lands. For many it was a second, third, or even fourth move since coming to America. These were frontiersmen and women, accustomed to the hardships of settlement, disease, Indian conflicts, and the elements. Those who set out before the Northwest Territory was officially opened knew that this circumstance would in time pose ownership problems. But they came nonetheless. They were also aware that the Indian tribes north of the Ohio River were desperately trying to discourage settlement on the lands granted to the English by the Iroquois south and east of the Ohio River in the Treaty of Fort Stanwick in 1768. Those native peoples who had not signed the treaty, including the Shawnee, were not resigned to the loss of their right to hunting grounds south of the Ohio River in the Kentucky country. But the lure of new and cheap land swept aside the fears of those seeking their dreams of personal freedom and land ownership. To these early peoples of the plains, forests, and swamps who had been deprived of land ownership or made slaves to the land in their home countries, no finer treasure could be had.

It appears that the Clawson extended families set out for the Fort Washington area in the New West from Greene County, Pennsylvania, a county in the extreme southwest corner of that state. The lands there are hilly and tree covered and abundant in streams. A drive through this country today is a delight; abundant streams, fragrant wild flowers, rolling tree covered hills, and charming little towns and churches set high apart present a picture postcard existence. But to the early squatter and settler it represented few opportunities for farming, and a reliance on mostly hunting and trapping for subsistence. For many of the Clawsons, who had purchased these lands originally at very little cost, the sales of their properties afforded them the opportunity to move on and purchase or claim large tracts of rich farm land further to the west. A small and beautiful mountain stream called Clawson's Run is all that remains in their beautiful mountain valley today to mark the lands they left behind.

Two branches of the Clawson family came to Ohio, that of Garrett Clawson and Cornelius Clawson. They were thought to be brothers

2

and sons of the first-generation immigrant, Garritt Klaassen. In all likelihood it was the descendants of Garrett who were first to arrive and settle at Columbia, Ohio, near Cincinnati. Garrett's sons Thomas, Peter, and Josiah can be authenticated as arriving with their widowed mother Mary in 1789. It appears that other family members from Greene County and other nearby locations may have traveled with Mary's family or shortly thereafter because great confusion has arisen over other persons named Thomas, John, Josiah, Frederick, and Peter who appear at various times in early mercantile, tax, and military records. It appears further that a sister named Mary arrived at Cincinnati in 1795 and a brother John in 1801. (For many years I was convinced from exhaustive research that our great-grandfather Josiah Clawson was the son of Thomas Clawson, one of the three brothers named above. However, more recent research has pointed out that he may have been instead a child of similar age born to another Thomas Clawson who lived out his last years in Allen County, Ohio.)

To further complicate matters, it appears from Ohio tax records of 1800-1810 and census records of 1820 that there were multiple Thomases, Josiahs, and Peters, in residence in Ohio. What we do know is that this family, like most early American families, tended to move together from place to place which makes perfect sense in terms of safety, economy, and support. It is highly unlikely with the scant documentation available in the Northwest Territory in those early days that we will ever be totally able to unravel these repetitive names.

Nothing has been recorded in the Clawson family history of the perils that Mary Clawson, her sons, and traveling companions may have endured on this journey.[2] However, it is well known from accounts of other travelers of this time period that there were frequent attacks on these flatboats from both sides of the River. Great animosity had grown amongst the Indians and whites over the taking of the traditional Indian hunting grounds in Kentucky by the Virginia forces under George Rogers Clark and by others who earlier still had ignored treaty agreements and become squatters and settlers on this fertile land. Flatboats were frequently attacked for the precious supplies they carried. Whites and Indians alike were killed and injured and captives were taken by both sides.

The year 1789 was the most dangerous year recorded for immigrant deaths on the Ohio River. However, it is estimated that in that one year alone 20,000 persons came down the Ohio River seeking new areas for settlement. In the previous seven years 1500 persons had died attempting their downstream journey to the new West. Somehow the Clawson group made it safely, first to Columbia, then, as Indian attacks increased, to Covalt Station, a fortification located at the site of what is now Terrace Park in northeast Cincinnati.

Most regrettably we lose track of Mary Clawson almost immediately upon her arrival in the Northwest Territory. There were no requirements that a woman, possibly living with grown children, needed to be noted by name in any way unless she purchased land on her own and paid taxes, or married. In the 1820, 1830, and 1840 Censuses, persons were listed only by sex and approximate age. Birth and death certificates were not required, and physicians who could have recorded such information were few, as were places of record. Indeed, although Ohio was established as a state in 1803, few death certificates can be found in the Ohio country issued before the middle and later part of the nineteenth century. Counties had to be established, courthouses built for storage and court proceedings, and laws enacted to govern the collection of matters pertaining to property transactions, wills, probate of wills, vital statistics, and criminal proceedings. Many early courthouses were of rough-hewn wood or log and were frequently subject to fire, flood, and other ravages of man and nature.[3]

Some very early churches kept records of their members; however, not all early settlers had the opportunity to attend even a most humble church, and if they did, chances are very slim that these records are to be found in the archives of the denomination today. The genealogist's best friend, if it has been preserved, is the family Bible. In it were recorded births, marriages and deaths. But again, there is a historical pitfall. Many early settlers in the new west were illiterate, and many of the documents that do exist were written by others for them and only signed with "The Mark Of" the person named in the text. It is very exciting to find a document actually signed by an ancestor or with a distinctive mark created by the signer, instead of just a simple "X."

Early families in America had a tradition of systematically naming their children in honor of other family members. To the genealogist this can be both a curse and a blessing. In the case of the Ohio Clawsons, the names are so often repeated that it takes years of research to find the proper thread of information to unravel. In many cases one cannot, no matter what the effort. On the other hand, this constant repeating of names helps one to identify the branch of the family to follow. In the case of the descendents of the Garrett and Cornelius lines, there is a distinct dissimilarity of first names, especially amongst the male members. Because of this, and for other reasons that will be explained later, it appears that the Josiah Clawson who settled in Putnam and Allen Counties in 1827-28 was a descendent of the Garrett Clawson line.

It is believed that the Clawson line in America extends back to Holland during that country's colonizing effort and its rule of New Amsterdam (New York) in the 1600s. The name Clawson has a wide variety of spellings in Holland, but all the variations are derivative of the name Nicholas. The most probable antecedent of the Garrett and Cornelius Clawson lines in America was Klaassen. The ending of "sen" is most typical of the southwest area of Holland.

It is generally accepted that the Clawson family heritage in America started sometime around the middle of the 1700s.[4] There are no connected records of the Clawson family which can be definitely established before the emergence of the second generation. There are only scattered notices relating to the original émigrés. Family stories handed down from year to year indicate that there were several family members who came to America together which is further evidenced by the fact that two other families had the same early history as ours: Cornelius Clawson, born in Holland in 1776, who settled in Pennsylvania then Ohio, and the Clawson family which settled in Jefferson County, Virginia (now West Virginia). It is probable that the Clawson families landed in Philadelphia and settled first in a colony with other passengers of their ship then each moved to other locations shortly after. There are no formal clues to their first settlement but there are available in Pennsylvania listings of land transactions for Thomas and Garrett Jr., in 1787, and tax records for Mary starting in 1781. Records also exist for Garrett Jr., of his participation in the Revolutionary War stating that he was born in

Greene County, Pennsylvania. Records indicate that Mary Clawson held land adjacent to three of her sons. Mary's husband, Garrett, appears to have died as the result of either defending his family or getting caught up in one of the many settler and Indian skirmishes that took place on the frontier, as so many soldiers and militiamen died in those early years.

The Clawsons, like many other early settlers, possibly came into southwest Pennsylvania (The District of West Virginia) from New Jersey and Maryland. Some migrated down the Shenandoah Valley, Berkeley, and Frederick Counties, Virginia, then via the Virginia Road, a crude trail hacked out of the wilderness. Others migrated across Southern Pennsylvania on the Pennsylvania Road, also a wilderness trail, which extended from Philadelphia to Lancaster to Pittsburgh. Numerous Indian trails also existed in Southwest Pennsylvania that could be followed if one wished to take the risk of traveling these well-known routes. Southwest Pennsylvania was the new frontier where land was cheap. Virginia also claimed the territory and encouraged her settlers to buy land with Virginia certificates at a very low price, whereas Pennsylvania offered the land at a much higher price. Because of boundary disputes, squatter's rights were honored, which meant the land was free to squatters until the disputes were settled. Therefore, settlers moved quite frequently, either claiming vacant land or trading for other squatter's claims. It was not uncommon to trade an old rifle for one or two hundred acres of land.

The earliest Clawsons to settle in the Pennsylvania area were possibly considered squatters as they had settled upon lands in the wilderness west of the Proclamation Line of 1763, which was established by the British to stem the tide of migration west of the Alleghenies. The Indian Territory past the crest of the Alleghenies was claimed by England. These frontiersmen were usually tough, proud, and persistent with a great capacity to endure. A piece of land meant more to them than the hardships of the wilderness, Indian raids, and disease, and they were willing endure all this and more for its acquisition.

It is believed that Garret Clawson, his wife Mary, and their children settled near Uniontown in what is Georges Township, Fayette County, Pennsylvania, in 1776. Garret was listed on the muster role of Gladdis' Command in the Monongalia Militia at Fort

Liberty, which was organized by Thomas Gaddis in September 1776. Fort Liberty was located about two miles south of Uniontown, the Clawson's home site. Later the family moved to the west side of the Monongahela River and settled on 100 acres near the western edge of Monongalia County, which became Greene Township, Washington County, then Greene County. (Pennsylvania had purchased this territory from the Indians in 1768 and named it Westmoreland County, but Virginia disputed the Pennsylvania authority and sent militia troops in to proclaim her own authority. Virginia forcefully retained jurisdiction during the Colonial period and erected the counties of Yohohania, Monongalia, and Ohio, in the District of West Augusta County, which included all the land west of the Allegheny Mountains.) Mary and her sons emigrated from here to Ohio. Presently, this location is about a mile east of the village of Jollytown, Pennsylvania.

Most of Garrett's and Mary's sons were in the military. Garrett Jr.. was drafted into the 13th Regiment of the Virginia Line, also known as the West Augusta Regiment, in May of 1778 and served one year. Peter Clawson served as an Indian Scout in Captain Stephen Gapen's Militia in 1782. John Clawson served in Captain John Guthery's Company of the Pennsylvania Militia in 1782. This service established a tradition that the Garrett Clawson family members would follow in the Ohio Country. Thomas, Peter, Josiah, and John became members of the Volunteer Militia after their arrival. Thomas reached the rank of Captain by 1804. In the War of 1812 he commanded a number of family members, from both the Clawson and Covalt families (his wife was Sophia Covalt).

Little is known of the lives of the Clawsons who possibly traveled with Mary's family or shortly thereafter. In the case of her son Thomas, who was a Baptist church member, military man, landholder, and mercantilist, records do exist that trace his activities in Ohio to 1824 when he and most of his family moved to Shawnee Township, Fountain County, Indiana. But information on the other extended family members who had relocated to the vicinity of Cincinnati are sadly lacking, as are details of their descendants' lives until at least thirty years later. Obviously, these are settlers busy carving lives out of the wilderness, not journal keepers or Bible recorders, and they may have been illiterate and unable to keep records had they wished to do so.

The tax rolls recorded in Ohio in the period 1800-1810 give us a glimpse of just how many adult landholding Clawson family members were in residence at that time. Listed were two Andrew Clawsons, one John, one Jonah, two Josiahs, two Peters, and three Thomases. All, it is assumed, were the descendants of Garret, Sr., or his brother, Cornelius, and as such were descendants of the patriarch of the family in America, Garritt Klaassen, and most, if not all, traveled together to the Ohio country or shortly after.

From the facts that were recorded concerning Thomas, Peter, and Josiah, we can make some basic assumptions about their extended families. Thomas and his brothers had doubtless heard while in Pennsylvania of the lands being opened in the Northwest Territory and for sale by John Cleve Symmes, who had badgered Congress into letting him lay claim to a million acres of land west of the Great Miami River in what was to later become the State of Ohio. His colleague in the venture, Major Benjamin Stites, promoted and sold these lands to hundreds of persons in Pennsylvania and the East. Many would later have to surrender their land, or re-purchase the acreages, because of governmental title disputes. The Clawson brothers were caught in this dilemma in 1799 when they had to sell their original holdings purchased from Symmes in 1797 and purchase others in a new location that had clear title. However, it appears that they prospered in these land exchanges. Thomas and his family moved to Indiana when the Treaty of St. Mary's, enacted in 1818, opened the Shawnee Indian lands there for sale. Again they were able to buy large tracts of cheap lands, based on the profits from the sale of their Ohio lands. (Before moving to Indiana in 1824, Thomas and his two brothers owned almost all of what now constitutes the city of Kettering, Ohio, a suburb of Dayton, Ohio.)

When the Clawsons arrived in 1789 at the site of the small settlement Losantiville (named by its surveyors based on its location) and nearby Fort Washington, General Arthur St. Clair, Governor of the Northwest Territory, had not yet arrived. St. Clair arrived to take up his command in 1790 and with great ceremony renamed Losantiville Cincinnati. (Many of the Revolutionary War veterans who had left their farms to fight identified with the Roman general and statesman Lucius Quinctius Cincinnatus and had formed a society dedicated in his honor of which George Washington was the first president and St. Clair a member.)

Fort Washington had been established in 1789 to protect the inhabitants of the Ohio River country who were downstream from Fort Harmer at Marietta and other lesser forts. It was a typical fort of that era, constructed of logs and inhabited by officers, enlisted men and their families, camp followers, traders, missionaries, and Indians who came and went. It is said that that the Shawnee warrior Tecumseh often visited Fort Washington to spy on the troops and learn of their plans for expansion north of the Ohio River. Settlers coming down the river would disembark at the fort, resupply, and split apart from their original group, either to claim land or to join others who had a particular destination in mind somewhere farther along. The Clawsons apparently went directly to Columbia, a settlement a bit north and east of Fort Washington, located at the mouth of the Little Miami River. (This is now the site of the Luken Airport.)

As to be expected, this sudden flood of immigrants and military personnel into the territory set aside for the Indians north of the Ohio River led to many bloody conflicts until 1795 when the Treaty of Greenville was signed, opening most of southern Ohio for settlement. For those Indians who did not consider themselves a part of that agreement, the battle to retain their hunting grounds was just beginning. Many of the Indian chiefs who signed the Greenville Treaty did so in good faith, believing that a peaceful settlement was their last hope for preserving the lives of their people, and they further firmly believed that the reservations granted to them would remain their homes, protected by the United States Government from white settlement. Sadly, this was not the case.

The Clawson families doubtless experienced many Indian raids on their settlements. For protection, they moved into Covalt Station[5] in 1790. (It is possible that the Clawsons and the Covalts had some prior knowledge of each other as both families came from Greene County, Pennsylvania.) Rightly or wrongly, these settlers had staked out their claims in this new territory, and many fought to the death to protect their families and home sites.

9

Covalt Station was founded by Abraham Covalt in January 1790, and was the farthest outpost in the Miami Purchase. Covalt granted a half-section of land at his cost to those who would join him and his family for mutual protection. Covalt Station was the scene of numerous Indian conflicts. In June of 1790, Abraham Covalt, Jr. was killed and scalped while hunting a few miles from the fort; shortly after, a friend of his was killed. In March of 1791 Abraham Covalt, Sr. and another man were killed and scalped just outside the walls of the fort. In all, nine settlers were killed or captured by Indians at the station before 1794. At one point, the attacks became so fierce and frequent that those remaining left Covalt Station and moved into Gerrard Station for protection, and many volunteered to fight with Generals Harmer and St. Clair in the battles to subdue the Native Americans and gain the lands for settlement north of the Ohio River. Covalt Station was re-occupied after the defeat of the Indians by General Anthony Wayne at the Battle of Fallen Timbers in 1794. It was later sold and eventually burned to the ground in 1810.

Abraham Covalt, the founder of Covalt Station, was quite a remarkable person who exhibited strong leadership qualities throughout his life.[6] Born in New Jersey in 1843, he was conscripted at eighteen by the British to take part in the Storming of Martinico. In 1772 he moved with his wife, Lois Pendleton, to Bedford County, Pennsylvania, where he continued his military service in the militia and the Continental Line. In 1777 he was elected Captain of the 6th Company, Second Battalion. In 1784 the Covalts moved to Greene County, Pennsylvania, to join other relatives there. While in Greene County, Covalt served as overseer of the poor and Supervisor of the Township. He and his family were devoted Baptists and attended Goshen Baptist Church in Greene County. Five years after his arrival in Greene County, he led a group of twelve family members and thirty-three friends down the Ohio River to establish new homes on the frontier. He traveled at least once to the Ohio County beforehand to select the site for the Station with Major Stites. It is possible that the Covalts as well as the Clawsons started their trip from Wheeling, Virginia, leaving first from Moundsville, a more direct route to the Ohio River from Greene County.

In her memoirs, Mary, daughter of Abraham Covalt Sr., tells a touching tale of the hardships of the frontier, the sudden violence of

Indian attacks and the death of loved ones.[7] Of the journey that took them down the Ohio River, she recounts, "The group left the first of January 1789 and arrived at the mouth of the Little Miami River the 19th of January 1789, at what is now called Columbia." The float trip was made in two flat bottom boats, one 55 feet in length, the other 40 feet; one boat carried the farm implements and 20 head of livestock, including cattle, swine, sheep, and 7 horses, and one boat carried millstones for a gristmill. One of the Greene County group was a millwright named Joseph Hinkle. A tent camp was set up at Columbia for the women and children while the men went up the Little Miami River to build a fort. The site selected for Covalt Station was at Round Bottom, twelve miles up the River from its mouth and a little below the present site of Milford, Ohio. This site at the confluences of the East Fork of the Little Miami River and the main river body was a natural one. It is believed to have been the first station erected in the Miami Valley.

The usual plan for a fort was a rectangle with cabins on the inner wall, with a blockhouse at each corner. However, Capt. Covalt modified the basic plan to protect the livestock. A drawing dated January 31st 1791 completed by Lieutenant Cornelius Sedam for General Harmer, Commander of Fort Washington, shows how the fort was modified with 17 cabins to a side and two areas for the livestock. This made a large structure covering 40,000 square feet and comparable in size to Fort Washington. A mill was constructed of round logs adjacent to the fort and a cemetery was set aside at a distance of 60 feet from the mill.

Thomas Clawson is repeatedly mentioned in the reminiscences of persons who lived at the Station. We can assume his prominence at the station was linked not only to his own efforts but also to the fact that he married Abraham Covalt's daughter, Sophia. However, there appears to more than one Thomas in the telling. For instance, the Thomas who fought with St. Clair's army and survived the slaughter at Fort Recovery to tell the tale appears not to be the Thomas who married Sophia. Also, there are tales of Thomas the remarkable marksman and Thomas the Indian fighter. One of the "Clawson" stories often repeated tells of an incident when a Clawson approached a blacksmith shop run by Edmund Munger to have some blacksmithing done but was told by Mr. Munger that he could not do the work as his family was out of fresh meat and he must go hunting for wild turkeys. Clawson is reported to have said, "I can kill more turkeys than you can, and if you'll go into the shop and do my work, I'll go into the woods and do your hunting." The blacksmith accepted the proposition, and Clawson with an old horse and a boy started into the woods. In the evening he returned and made good his boast, for on the old horse was loaded twenty–one fine fat turkeys.[8] Other reminiscences of the time relate to a "Thomas" who was a fine hunter, fighter, and companion. One gets the distinct feeling that there was Thomas, son of Mary, who was a military man, land speculator, merchant, and public servant, and that the other two Thomases who turn up on the early tax rolls were, if not younger, at least freer spirits living the adventurous life of the frontier.

In the 1820 Ohio Census three Thomas Clawsons are listed: two in Montgomery County and one in Ross County. All appeared to be close in age at 45 and older. In the 1830 Census only one Thomas age 60 and older remained to be recorded. This Thomas lived in Allen County, Ohio, next door to a young Josiah, Frederick, and Andrew Clawson. By 1840 this Thomas had disappeared from the census as well.

Notes

[1] The Charles Clawson manuscript *Thomas Clawson and Allied Families* was extremely helpful in establishing the history and environment of the Clawsons who emigrated from Pennsylvania to the Ohio Country. On a research trip to southwest Pennsylvania in the mid-1990s, I discovered the actual sites of the farms the Clawsons left behind as well as the charming little stream called Clawson's Run. The Clawsons' homes in the flatlands of central and northern Ohio differed greatly from the high, tree-covered hills they left behind. Quite unexpectedly in the late 1990s, an unpublished manuscript by a Mrs. George Dinwiddie of West Lafayette, Indiana, was forwarded to me by a New Jersey researcher of the Covalt family. It brought some new insights relating to the migrations of the Clawsons, first to Pennsylvania and then to Ohio.

[2] Early in my research I reached out to the research department of the Cincinnati Museum Center. This contact became invaluable over the years. Tax rolls, military enrollment, census figures, mercantile records, and first hand accounts of the experiences of early Ohio settlers – these are just some of the valuable materials that I requested and received. There is a fee for research, of course, but it is reasonable and prompt. For those who wish to read further of the perils of travel on the Ohio River, an old and a recent book are highly recommended: Banta's *The Ohio* and Eckert's *That Dark and Bloody River*. Both books have excellent bibliographies for further reading.

[3] The material on the history of the courthouse in Ohio was drawn from my Master of Fine Arts thesis completed in 1964 at Bowling Green State University, Ohio entitled *A Study of Extant Courthouses Built in Ohio 1830-1860*. For many years the history of courthouse architecture that I had prepared for this manuscript was the only one available to Ohio courthouse researchers. In the early 1980s the historical material cited above plus a number of my courthouse descriptions were included in a volume prepared for the Ohio County Commissioners Association entitled *Development of Ohio's Counties and Their Historic Courthouses*.

[4] The Clawson material is largely drawn from the Charles Clawson and Mrs. Dinwiddie manuscripts and research materials passed on to me from an elderly cousin, Olen Fosnaugh, now deceased. Olen Fosnaugh's mother Monna was our paternal grandmother's sister. Olen did his research over many years while seeking an ancestor he could authenticate having fought in the Revolutionary War. He managed to be accepted to The Sons of the American Revolution by his link to Leinert Hire (Heyer), Elizabeth's Hire's great-grandfather. (Elizabeth was Josiah Clawson's second wife.) More recent research has shown that a number of other avenues are now open to Clawson descendents who wish to join the Daughters or Sons of the American Revolution.

[5] The book *Descendents of Covalt, Covault, Cavolt, Their History and Genealogy in America 1714-1900* gives an excellent account of the

building of Covalt Station and the activities of its inhabitants at the beginning of the nineteenth century.

[6] For those interested in the life and times of Abraham Covalt and his descendents, the book *Descendents of Covalt, Covault, Cavolt, Their History and Genealogy in America 1714-1900* (also cited above) is an excellent resource.

[7] Mary Covalt's memoir is repeated in the volume *Descendents of Covalt, Covault, Cavolt, Their History and Genealogy in America 1714-1900* and is also on file with the Cincinnati Museum Center.

[8] *Beers History of Montgomery County, Ohio* is credited with the "Clawson Hunter" story; however, it also available in its original form from the Cincinnati Museum Center.

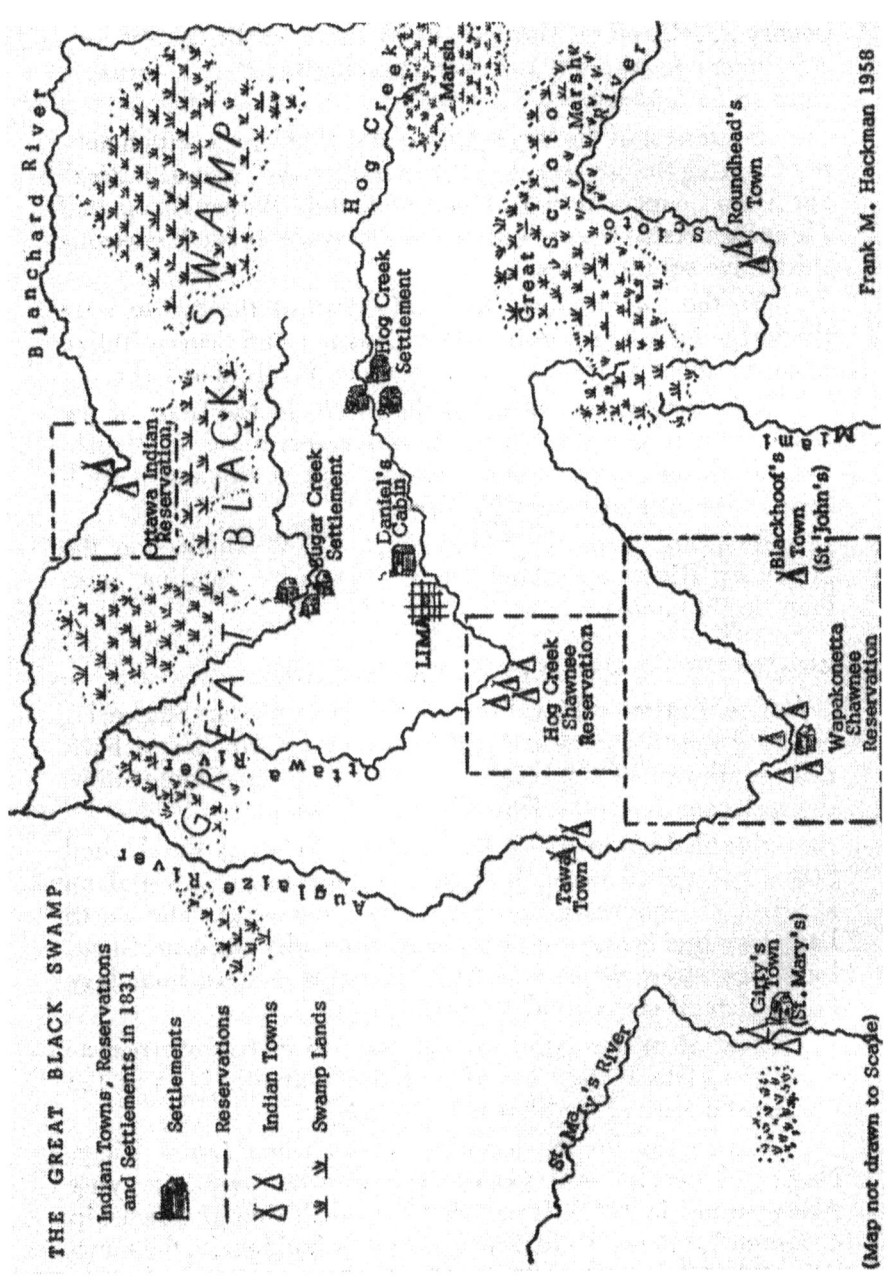

Map courtesy of Allen County Museum, Lima, Ohio.

Chapter Two: 1828, Coming to Northwest Ohio

In the spring of 1828 our great-great-grandfather Josiah Clawson[1] joined a group of former United States Army officers and enlisted men who had commandeered and taken up residence in the blockhouse of Fort Amanda[2] on the Auglaize River in Northwestern Ohio. Many at the fort planned to eventually take possession of lands granted to them by President Andrew Jackson for their service in the War of 1812 or to purchase lands released for sale obtained by the United States government through Indian Treaties. Many of the earliest fort arrivals in 1817 were undoubtedly familiar with the fort, either having been stationed at the fort or having spent time at the fort hospital or ship-building facility during the War of 1812.

Plaque on Fort Amanda monument showing image of original fort of 1812 built on this site.

Monument erected at the site of Fort Amanda, built in 1812 on a bend of the Auglaize River in northwestern Ohio.

A short distance from the Fort on the banks of the river rested an Ottawa Indian village called Tawa. A few miles east of the Tawa village there was a Shawnee settlement village called Hog Creek and further east and south situated on the Auglaize River was the village of Wapakoneta, the home village of Black Hoof, principal Chieftain of the Shawnee Indians. Connecting the Hog Creek Indian village to Wapakoneta was a trail laid out by the revered Shawnee Indian Quilna, who was said to have the rare gift of "seeing from above." Eventually part of this trail became Elm Street, the main thoroughfare of the new community of Lima, founded in 1831, which encompassed much of what had been Shawnee lands and settlements.

The Hog Creek Shawnees, through tradition and treaty, also owed their allegiance to Chief Black Hoof. Various treaties drawn between the United State government and the tribes of the Ohio Country had granted specified reserves in the Northwest corner of Ohio. Treaties were made at St. Mary's in 1818 with all remaining Shawnees, Ottawas, Wyandots, Senecas, Weas and Miamis. A number of large tracts of land had also been granted after the War of 1812 to individuals who had served as Indian scouts and spies. These men had assisted the United States Army in its battle with the British and in defeating the great Shawnee leader Tecumseh in his struggle to unify the tribes and push back white emigration into the Midwest.

The previous Treaty of St. Mary's in 1817 executed "at the foot of the rapids of the Maumee" had set aside a 25-square-mile tract of land in the northwest corner of Ohio for the use of the Shawnee in perpetuity. Flowing through this reservation was the Auglaize River, which had been a lifeline for the Shawnee, Ottawa, Wyandot, Seneca, and others traveling north and south from Lake Erie to the Ohio River. Bordering the Shawnee Reserve was the area known as The Great Black Swamp.[3] To the Indians in the past it was a dark, dank, and deep area that could be passed through and around with some ease, but to the white settler who wished to claim these fertile lands for settlement and farming it was an enormous hazard and impediment. All who attempted to permanently occupy this tract in the 1820s found the land was a dangerous force to be conquered and lived with. The constant battle with malaria caused by great swarms of mosquitoes emanating from the swamp water devastated native people and immigrants alike.

In the past only the French fur traders, native hunters, the occasional wandering missionary, or the land-seeking squatter had sought to occupy this swampy wooded land, usually only temporarily or in small numbers. With the end of the War of 1812, this quiet land began to change dramatically. Villages and towns sprang up as if by magic. Land was drained, ditches dug, and canals built to facilitate travel between the main rivers and streams. Native tribes and non-Indians began to live side-by-side, engaging in day-to-day living and commercial activities. It was an exciting and dangerous time for both.

In the thirty-two years between the signing of the Greenville Treaty and the recording of our great-great-grandparents' wedding in Shelby County in 1823, life along the rivers and streams of Northwest Ohio was largely a peaceable time. Indians and settlers alike were busy with many of the same tasks. To be sure, the various tribal members still journeyed with their families on the winter hunts, but they also came back to their villages and towns to build substantial homes, grow their crops and tend the graves of their ancestors. Wapakoneta, the council headquarters of the Shawnee under Chief Black Hoof, became a thriving settlement on the Auglaize River and the focus of the efforts of Henry Harvey, a Quaker, who with Eastern Quaker support financed setting up a mill there.[4] The Quakers encouraged farming and cattle-raising and provided the start-up monies for these efforts as well as blacksmithing and other trades. The various Indian notables, including Tecumseh, attended Council meeting at Wapakoneta as they traveled up and down the Auglaize. Chief PHT also built a council house near the settlement of Lima. Tragically, PHT died shortly before its completion and only a short time before the Shawnees were forced to leave their reservation for Kansas in 1832-33. PHT was buried by his people with great ceremony near the Council House. All who attended, Indian and settler, were impressed with the ritual and solemnity of the occasion. Details of PHT's funeral ceremony were passed on in word and print by those who had witnessed the event long after the Council House had become ruins.

We can only assume that in Ohio during the early nineteenth century the original Clawson émigrés had settled in and had families and that the older family members who had chosen to stay in Ohio now had offspring who had households of their own. There were 19 Clawson households listed in the 1820 Census, 22 in 1830, and 22 in 1840. By the time of the 1850 Census, when names and exact ages were listed for household members, there were a total of 30 households, and in 1860 just before the Civil War there were 73. The constant repetition of names seems to have dissipated somewhat by 1850, however, and the Clawsons remained largely clustered in the central and north central counties. The boundaries of these counties kept shifting about until they finally settled into their permanent locations around 1850. These shifting boundaries create a bit of confusion for the researcher, but in general the Clawsons did not stray far from the locations they chose when these counties were first opened for settlement. It is painfully clear that descendants of these families, countrywide now, spend countless hours trying to decipher which Peter, which Thomas, which Josiah, which Rachel, which Andrew, and so on. No matter how persistent, one must finally come to terms with this dilemma, say, "This is the ancestor that I do know about with some surety," and start from there.

In the case of our family, that is Josiah Clawson, who came to Allen and Putnam Counties in 1828. And there our Clawson story begins.

Notes

[1] Josiah Clawson's arrivals at Fort Jennings and Fort Amanda are noted in the *History of Allen County* and the *1888 History and Atlas of Putnam County, Ohio*. These two publications, plus mention in other area histories, establish Josiah as one of the first white settlers in both Jennings and Marion Townships. His first purchase of land was in the area of the old Fort Jennings. Before the sale of his holdings in Putnam County, he purchased land in Allen County further up the Auglaize River. He and his family members quite possibly squatted on this land several years before it was released for formal purchase as they are listed on the federal census in 1830 as being in this location.

[2] The site of Fort Amanda is preserved to this day as an Ohio State Park located on Route 198 outside Lima, Ohio. The park, situated on a beautiful bend of the Auglaize River, also includes a cemetery for the seventy-five unknown soldiers buried there as well as the graves of early settlers of the area. A fifty-foot granite obelisk monument at the site of the old fort was dedicated in 1915 to the brave men who had died in the War of 1812. A bronze plaque on the side of the monument depicts the fort as it was seen, described and sketched in 1812.

---

[3] Frank W. Hackman's *It Happened Here: Portraits of the Great Black Swamp* is an excellent source for a short history of this area. Although the fields were drained and the trees removed long ago, the soil is still an inky black and highly fertile. It is an area ideal for growing vegetables and as such became a valuable resource to the nation during both World War I and World War II. The need for field workers during those times was responsible for a population shift from the southern states to the Lima area and many families stayed on after the wars to become permanent members of their chosen communities.

[4] Henry Harvey's *History of the Shawnee Indians, From the Year 1681 to 1854, Inclusive* is a must-read for anyone seeking firsthand knowledge of the lives of the Shawnee along the Auglaize River in the early years of the nineteenth century. Not only did Harvey live and work with the Shawnee in Wapakoneta, but he also followed them to their new homes in Kansas and eventually set up new missions for them in the West. All Indian affairs during this time were housed in the War Department and Harvey's book chronicles the treaties, the allotments, and the sale of the Shawnee Indian lands in detail. The Shawnee were paid pitifully little for their lands in Ohio, and spent many years after their Removal in attempts to be paid what they had been promised by the War Department. Some monies were never recovered and many promises made to them were never kept.

Chapter Three: Fort Amanda

Nothing is known about our great-great-grandfather Josiah Clawson before 1823 when it was recorded in Shelby County, Ohio, that he had obtained a license to marry a Mary Russell.[1] His birth date was not recorded at that time nor was his age at his death in 1844. (Taking into account various historical documents, it is believed that his birth date was around 1800.) At this writing, the evidence available would lead one to conclude that he was the son of the Thomas with whom he came to Fort Amanda in 1828. Thomas and Josiah are not names commonly used by the descendants of Cornelius Clawson, but the descendants of Garret Clawson repeated these names through many generations. That our Josiah's father was named Thomas can be reasonably surmised from the fact that he and Frederick and an older Thomas Clawson arrived at Fort Amanda together. They all became neighbors along the banks of the Auglaize River and were joined shortly thereafter by Andrew Clawson, Mercy Clawson Kiggins, and Rachael Clawson Patton.

Josiah still held land holdings in Shelby County when he died and apparently was the first in his family to purchase land in both Putnam and Allen Counties shortly after he arrived at Fort Amanda.[2] He purchased his first parcel of land at Fort Jennings, an 1812 fort downriver approximately twenty miles from Fort Amanda. In 1834 he sold this large tract of land on the Auglaize River to a group of newly arrived German immigrants. This parcel of land included the fort site and became the nucleus for the charming village of Fort Jennings, which exists to this day. The formal deed to his second purchase upriver from Fort Jennings was officially registered and signed by President Andrew Jackson in 1831. The historical atlases of both Allen and Putnam Counties list him as being one of the first white men to settle in each. Josiah contributed a good deal to both of these communities of settlers, as he was a merchant, farmer, and public servant of Jennings Township.

In 1831 another Josiah Clawson family came to settle in nearby Auglaize County, not far from the first group. This Josiah was a bit younger than Thomas, but it is possible that both this Josiah and Thomas were brothers or at least close relatives. The Probate of our great-great-grandfather's estate in 1845 indicates that there were business and personal connections between these two families, but no legal records that would confirm blood kinship have been found at this time. Most compelling for an assumption of kinship is the similarity of names running through both families and the fact that within three years of the Thomas family's arrival this family arrived to settle nearby. No other Clawson families came to settle in the Allen, Putnam, or Auglaize County areas in the early nineteenth century.

In any event, these settlers were some of the first non-Indian landholders to purchase land that was supposed to remain the perpetual Reserves granted to the Native Americans by treaty in 1817 and 1818. (The federal government, through its agents during the years 1830 – 1832, negotiated the sale of the Indian lands provided for in the Treaties of St. Mary's, thereby opening these lands for purchase.) In all cases, these early settlers became the close neighbors, and often close friends, of the Native Americans whose lands they now occupied. Only a few decades earlier, these same families had been locked in mortal combat with members of the same native tribes, a fact that must have seemed remarkable to native and non-native alike.

When Josiah and his wife Martha arrived at Fort Amanda in 1828, they had been married five years and had a small daughter named Jinky, after Martha's younger sister. Martha's parents, Andrew Russell and Elizabeth Sunderland, were the first squatters to settle at Fort Amanda in 1817, and they had experienced many hardships in the years before Martha and Josiah's arrival.[3]

Fort Amanda had been commissioned by General Anthony Wayne to defend against the Auglaize and Ottawa River Indians during the War of 1812. From September 1, 1812, until late in the fall of that year, General William Harrison had his headquarters at Fort St. Mary's. In the late fall of that year Colonel Thomas Poague was ordered to clear and construct a wagon road through the wilderness from St. Mary's to Defiance, Ohio. The road was completed sometime during October, and the regiment returned to a point on the west bank of the Auglaize River where they erected a fort, which Poague named Amanda in honor of his wife.

Fort Amanda became a base of supplies for the armies of the Maumee Valley. Many of General Harrison's orders were dispatched from here, and the office of the paymaster of the army was located at the fort. The hospital within the stockade was erected in the spring of 1813 and soon was filled with sick and wounded soldiers brought by boat from the battlefields along the Maumee River. Many of the men stationed here had also served in the Revolutionary War and the Border Wars of Western Pennsylvania. The soldiers who died at the fort were buried north of the fort near a ravine. Sadly, no records exist of those who may have fallen here as all records of the fort were destroyed when the national capitol was burned by the British.

During the winter of 1812-13, a shipbuilding company was constructed east of the fort on the river. Seventy-five boats were constructed at the fort by members of the militia and troops from Fort Winchester. Twelve hundred men embarked from the fort to reinforce the troops at Fort Miegs, near present-day Toledo. The battle at Fort Miegs in 1813 was one of the last great battles led by the Shawnee warrior chief Tecumseh in his efforts to unite all Indians against the incursion on their native lands. Others of the boats were used to assist Commodore Perry in buoying his larger vessels over the shallows in Put-in-Bay on the day of his celebrated victory over the British and Native American forces. At the close of the war in 1814, the troops were mustered out of service and the stockade and blockhouses left tenantless until three years later with the arrival of the Russell family.[4]

When the Russells arrived at Fort Amanda in 1817, Northwest Ohio was a true wilderness. Heavy forests, wild animals, and deep and dark swamps covered the land. Most travel was done on the rivers and overland traces that followed the rivers and on well-worn Indian trails. The great Shawnee warrior Tecumseh, his Indian supporters, and British allies had just four years before they would fight and lose a great battle against the Americans at the River Thames in Canada. For many years Tecumseh had rallied the Indian tribes in the Midwest and South to join together and to push the whites out and back to the East. But the tide of Americans into the Midwest proved to be too strong even for this mighty and inspirational warrior. Black Hoof's people along the Auglaize River resisted joining forces with Tecumseh, guided by Black Hoof's belief that co-existence was their key to survival. When Tecumseh died in the Battle of Thames in 1813 the die was cast. All hope of fighting back was crushed. The old warrior chiefs from this region – Roundhead, Blue Jacket, Black Hoof, and others – had been either killed or beaten into submission by governmental maneuvering. By the time the War of 1812 was over, it was apparent that these Indian Reserves would eventually be taken over by the government and that land-hungry immigrants would waste no time in squatting on what was by treaty Indian lands.

Martha Russell's parents, Andrew Russell and Elizabeth Sunderland, had preceded the Clawsons to Fort Amanda by a full decade. The Russells arrived at the Fort in 1817 coming from Montgomery County near Dayton. Andrew had been stationed at Fort Jennings during the War of 1812 and would have been familiar with the facilities at Fort Amanda, which were far superior to the quarters at Fort Jennings. They took possession of the fort property and set up housekeeping in the deserted officer's headquarters. Very shortly, others came to join them with their families, including two of Elizabeth's brothers.

Although it is known that the Russells migrated from New Jersey to Ohio, the first record of Andrew and Elizabeth is their marriage in Belmont County in 1803. Andrew died at Fort Amanda in 1822. Martha was not named in her father's will but was listed as purchasing some items from his estate. This circumstance would perhaps indicate that Martha lived at a distance from her parents, or perhaps that there was some estrangement in their relationship. The move to Allen County may indicate that after Martha's marriage to Josiah in Shelby County in 1823 there was a wish on their part to be near Martha's mother and siblings. Martha's widowed mother was left with five daughters and a son to rear. A daughter, Susanna, born to the Russells shortly after their arrival at the Fort had the distinction of being the first white child to be born in what was then Allen County, Ohio.

The Russell's son Joseph, in a narrative written many years later, recounts the hardships and pleasures of their early years at the fort:

> The first four years, we were sick most of the time;
> on one occasion the second year there, we were all so
> ill at the same time we could not feed one another –

probably would have starved to death had it not been for the Indians. They came and fed us and ministered to our wants and needs best they knew how. They were always very kind to us. My playmate as a boy was an Indian lad, in fact, most of my playmates were Indian, I learned their ways – could make a bow and arrow with the best of them, could shoot with them, and our amusements consisted mostly of shooting at a target and wrestling.

The only white visitor I remember ever having, for years when I was small, was Duchoquette, a French Indian trader. He taught me to read and to count in the French tongue. The first school I attended was during the winter of 1821. Father took me on horse back to Grandfather Sunderland's in the fall and came for me in the spring. (*Author's note*: Joseph would have been seven years old.)

Our main foodstuffs were Johnny cake and corn meal mush.

The first wheat we raised was cut with a sickle, a hooked shaped knife, and threshed with a flail. When I was five years old, Father put two sacks of wheat on one horse; he rode another putting me in front of him, and traveling in this way, we went to Grandfather Peter Sunderland's place in Montgomery County. There was a horse mill down there where we went to have the wheat ground. We used our two horses to turn this mill.

Father was very ill that summer and died in the fall. Mother then took the horses to Dayton, packed them with packs of food for the winter on their backs, and walked back home leading the horses. With the goods at hand she opened a store and traded with the Indians. When she got enough furs to warrant the trip, she would take them on horses, borrow another horse from one of my Uncles, and go to Dayton, getting more goods in exchange for furs and returning to replenish the stock of her little store.

In this age of superhighways and comfortable means of travel, it is hard to imagine traveling sixty or seventy miles by horseback over primitive trails to have a few sacks of wheat ground into flour or to secure supplies for one's own family to use or to resell. It is harder still to imagine that a small child would be taken such a distance to live with relatives in order to attend school from fall to the following spring. Northwest Ohio was still very much an untamed wilderness when Josiah, Martha, and other Clawson family members arrived at the fort in 1827-28.

But there were pleasant and happy times as well. The Shawnee Indians continued to be friends of the Fort families and assisted them in seeking out the best lands for their farms and future settlements. When the renowned Shawnee Chief Pe-Aitch-ta (PHT) died, his family gave Andrew Russell a pony for his help in preparing the Chief's grave. It is said that this pony lived to the great age of twenty-eight years and served the family well. Many stories are recorded in old county histories of western Ohio of the sharing and kindness that took place between the Native and non-native peoples of the Auglaize River area. To be sure, there were isolated tragic incidents, but in the late 1820s and 1830s both groups were absorbed with their survival in this corner of the wilderness.

Joseph Russell recalls with great fondness the many times he spent with John Chapman (better known as Johnny Appleseed):

> He had a nursery south of the Fort. He was always very kind to me; used to teach me a lot about the Bible. I used often to go and help him with his work. He was a very peculiar man – he would eat with us, but we never could get him to sleep in the house. He would sleep on the ground, under a tree no difference what the weather was. He always said that God took care of him. He made his own clothes out of his appleseed sacks. He let his hair grow long and never wore a hat. I have seen him sit with the mosquitoes just swarming about him and biting him, yet he would never kill one, saying that God had put them on earth for some reason,

that it was wicked to kill any of God's creatures. He never ate meat of any kind.

Not all of Joseph's spiritual training came so gently. His first brush with organized religion left a lasting impression.

> The first religious service I remember was held at our place at Fort Amanda where Peter Cartwright preached on occasion. I well recall the occasion of his first visit there. I got up early, went out back of the blockhouse and was cracking some hickory nuts. Cartwright came out and told me how wicked I was for doing that on Sunday. He told me I would sure go to Hell if I was not a good boy; in fact he then and there preached me a sermon.

Shortly after the Russell family squatted at Fort Amanda, they were joined by the family of Martin Hire.[5] The Hire family would in time have nine children. When they arrived at Fort Amanda, their baby daughter Elizabeth, who was born July 14, 1817, in Fayette County, Ohio, was just a toddler.

The progenitor of the Hire family in America was Leonard Hire (Lienert Heyer) who came from Switzerland in 1737. His son, Leonard Jr., was ten years old at the time. By 1750 the Hires had settled first in Pennsylvania and then removed to the South Branch Valley of the Potomac, near the present town of Petersburg, West Virginia. It is the grandson of this Leonard, Leonard Hire III, who is the father of Martin Hire, Elizabeth's father. Leonard Hire III was in the Company of Ensign Stephen Ashby in 1775 during the Revolutionary War. He was later held captive by Indians for three years in Ohio. The location of his captivity is thought to have been in either Ross or Fayette Counties. Leonard Jr., had fought during the French and Indian War and his father, Leonard Sr., furnished supplies for the troops at that time. It is not surprising, given this family's history of military involvement, that Martin Hire was engaged in the War of 1812. He came to Fort Amanda expecting to be granted Bounty Lands as compensation for his service during the War. The Hires and the Russells were soon joined by other friends and comrades who anticipated more Indian lands being open to settlement by treaty and purchase.

Martin Hire was born in Virginia circa 1792, but perhaps emigrated to Ross County, Ohio, with his family at an early age. He was married in that county to Sally Neely on August 14, 1811. The Hires did not stay long at Fort Amanda but relocated to land near the village of Moulton in Auglaize County. Martin was a farmer, carpenter, and cabinetmaker. Sally died sometime after 1831 and before 1847 as Martin remarried in 1847 to Phebe Bates who was twenty years his junior. In the period between Sally's death and his re-marriage, he petitioned for and received Bounty Lands about a half-mile from Fort Amanda on the Auglaize River. He died June 10, 1851, and is buried in the Hartshorn Cemetery at the river's edge alongside his family members, fellow soldiers, and Indian neighbors.

Sometime before 1833 Martha Russell Clawson died leaving her young daughter Jinky to be reared by her widowed husband, Josiah. As was the custom in those times, the husband soon remarried, and, as it was also widely accepted in the early nineteenth century, the widower Josiah married a very young woman – Elizabeth, the sixteen-year-old daughter of Martin Hire. Over the next eleven years the couple had five children: Lauretta, born in 1834; William, 1837; Martha L., 1839; Sarah, 1842; and Josiah, Jr., a month after his father's death in 1844. This child born at so sad a time would become our great-grandfather. The Russell connection had led the Clawsons to Allen and Putnam Counties, but it was the Fort Amanda connection that brought together the elements of our ancestry.

It is not known for a certainty just how long the Clawsons stayed at the Fort, but it is apparent from the 1830 Census records that Josiah, Frederick, Thomas, and Andrew now had households of their own on what became known as the Defiance Trail, a winding road which followed the path of the Auglaize River downstream. The site of Josiah's home, farm and store stretched along the Auglaize River north of the former 30N, now called the Lincoln Highway, and considerably south of the highway along the river, as well. Across the road from the site of the family home rests the small Hartshorn Cemetery, where many of our ancestors are buried. Although the land appears to have been part of the original Clawson purchase, the cemetery is named after the Clawsons' near neighbors, the

Hartshorns. The reason for this is undoubtedly that the Hartshorns purchased a parcel of land from the Josiah Clawson estate in 1847 and set aside a small portion of it along the river for a family cemetery.

When Josiah died unexpectedly in 1844, his pregnant widow Elizabeth and the surviving children were left with numerous landholdings and possessions to dispose of, as Josiah had not filed a will. Josiah was Clerk of Jennings Township and a member of the School Board. These legal materials needed to be turned over to the County authorities. In addition, he operated a store where many materials were on consignment. His landholdings in Shelby, Putnam, and Allen Counties needed to be disposed of, obligations paid and consignment materials returned. William Scott, attorney and surveyor, was appointed administrator of his estate and Attorneys Edward Hartshorn and his son Elmore were named the executors. Apparently the Clawsons and the Hartshorns were trusted friends as well as neighbors, and it is a fair assumption that the children of both families knew each other well. Elizabeth Hire Clawson and her children were left with sufficient means but no father to guide their progress. Elizabeth remarried to David Whirrett and they added four children to the Hire/Clawson brood. The Clawson children complained bitterly in later years that they had not been dealt with fairly or treated well by the stepfather who had, in their opinions, "inherited" their father's estate.

The Hartshorn family was held in high esteem in the Auglaize River communities by both Indians and whites. Edward came with his family to Bath Township in Allen County in the early 1830s, possibly directly from Knox County, Ohio. In addition to being an attorney, Edward may have also been somewhat of a land speculator. Edward was born to George and Hannah Hartshorn in 1793 in Grog Town, Duck Creek Hundred, Kent County, Delaware. Land speculation may have been in Edward's blood as prior to 1810 his family had come to Marietta, Ohio, on the Ohio River, as a result of the development of the Ohio Land Company. He and his brothers became prominent members of the Marietta community and were involved in the land transactions that established Marietta and the fortifications there. Numerous land tractions took place over the years between the Hartshorn family and General Rufus Putnam, who with others had

31

founded the Ohio Land Company in 1787, shortly after the passage of the Northwest Ordinance.

In his excellent and comprehensive book *The Hartshorn Families in America*, Derrick S. Hartshorn, III, chronicles the Hartshorns from the progenitor Thomas Hartshorn who settled in Reading, Massachusetts, in 1634 having come from the area of Derbyshire, England, and a town named Hartshorn. The line of the George Hartshorn family is believed to have come to America in 1780-1790. (George was not a popular name in the Colonies until around 1790.) At present, it is thought that the "George" line of ancestry in Ohio can be traced back to 1200. For anyone who has the surname Hartshorn in the family, the above book can be recommended as a well- researched source.

As befit a young attorney and member of a founding family, on January 12, 1815 Edward married another member of a founding family in Marietta, Lydia DeLong.[6] Jonathan and Margaret DeLong, Lydia's parents, were founding members of Salem Township, Washington County, in 1795. Lydia had been born two years earlier in Center County, Pennsylvania. Lydia's father served in the Northumberland Militia during the Revolutionary War and was held prisoner, for which he received compensation from the government in 1791. Lydia's father died in 1814 leaving her an inheritance. Although Edward and Lydia may have left Marietta sometime before 1824, it appears that his brothers stayed on and contributed substantially to the development of the Marietta community. His father removed to Jefferson County where he died December 25, 1829, naming Edward in his will as the recipient of a horse and saddle.

Elmore was born to Edward and Lydia in 1816. It is not known when Lydia died, but it is known that Edward remarried in 1824. Edward remarried, at least once, to a Mary Cramer (also known as Polly) on January 22, 1824 in Knox County, Ohio.[7] This marriage is further evidenced by the disparity of ages of his children listed in the 1850 Allen County Census. He and Mary engaged in numerous land transactions in both Knox and Allen Counties. His eldest son, by Lydia, became a lawyer like his father, and others of his children became professionals in other fields. As mentioned, Edward became a Justice of the Peace and a judge, and, in addition to his judicial duties, he conducted marriage ceremonies for many couples in the area throughout his lifetime. From all accounts, he was a good and fair man, vitally interested in his family and the communities where he settled. Further, he was a man of no small means who engaged often in the exchange of properties.

The cast of our ancestry was slowly falling into place along the banks of the Auglaize River in the northwest corner of Ohio. When the Russells, Hires, Clawsons, and Hartshorns first arrived, they were squatting on land not yet formally released for settlement, just as the older generation had done in the Ohio River area. The forts along the Auglaize that they gravitated to were built and maintained under the command of the federal government to house and provision solders and protect newly arrived settlers during the War of 1812. The war was long over and the old forts of little use except to house the temporary squatter or to provide materials for building elsewhere. Little by little and piece by piece, the native peoples were being crowded in and squeezed out by the new immigrants. Meanwhile, friendships had been forged, dependencies built and old animosities put away. It is heartbreaking to realize as these early settlers were living amongst the native population, engaging in commerce with them, being guided in the ways of the wilderness by them, and even being saved from disease and hunger by them, that their very presence was speeding the forced departure of the Native Americans – not by guns and armed defeat as it had been three decades earlier, but by laws and treaties enacted by the federal government.

The Frenchman Duchoquette, of whom Joseph Russell wrote, was a true friend to the Shawnee Indians and acted as an interpreter for them at Wapakoneta in their negotiations with the federal agents over the release of their lands. Duchoquette was shocked and infuriated when he heard the deceptive language and insinuations used by the agents to secure the Shawnee lands at an unbelievably low price. He took it upon himself to go to Washington by horseback with a group of Indian chiefs and friendly Quakers to plead the Shawnees case for fairness and truth. Unfortunately, Duchoquette was taken grievously ill along the way and died.[8] Bereft of friends who could plead their case, the Shawnees lost their lands and were forced to leave their homeland for Kansas in the West by 1832.

Black Hoof, the wise and noble chief who was also once a great warrior who fought fiercely against white encroachment, died in 1831, shortly before the last of his people were removed from Wapakoneta and the Shawnee Reserve. He was buried with ceremony at the cemetery at St. John's, a village only a few miles from his tribal center at Wapakoneta. At St. John's a monument has been erected to him by his people near the site of his little home. Other Indian tribes of the area – the Wyandots, Ottawas, Delawares, Seneca, and others – were all removed from northwestern Ohio by 1842. Only those too ill to travel or with no one to care for them were allowed to stay for a time. Some few hid away in the hills of southern Ohio, Indiana, and Illinois, eventually blending in with other ethnic groups, but some, if not all, held quietly to their own cultures and ways.

Almost a hundred years after the fact, Frank Burkhardt, author of the 1928 newspaper clipping cited below, manages to convey some of the pathos surrounding the removal of the Shawnee from Northwest Ohio.[9] Many stories concerning the Shawnee Removal were mentioned in old Allen and Auglaize County histories. The Removal left a deep impression on the early settlers as they watched from the side of the roadways as their old friends and neighbors were being led away. Surely, stories must have been passed down through many generations about this and other experiences that they shared with the Shawnee. My father, who was born in 1905, remembered that his father told him how in the late 1800s the Indians would still come and walk the banks of the Auglaize River to visit the burial grounds of their ancestors. Although seldom spoken of, my Shawnee friends assure me that this ritual is still practiced.

In September 1831, the repulsive Gardner (Indian Commissioner who arranged sale of Shawnee lands) came to Wapakoneta accompanied by a West Point Cadet to arrange for the journey to Kansas. The young man made a flowery speech in which he urged that the route to Kansas be by way of Urbana and Lebanon, Ohio. The chiefs held council and it was decided to go by way of Greenville, Ohio, and Richmond and Indianapolis, Indiana. When the great family leveled the graves and started the long journey in November 1832, they traveled the route selected by the chiefs.

The Hog Creek tribe of the Shawnee did not make the journey until the following spring. Allen County had some 500 settlers by this time and many mingled socially with the Shawnees and became warm friends. For several weeks (before departure) there were ceremonies and dances. The graves were covered with sod so as to be unmarked. They bid adieu to the waters of Hog Creek where they had paddled their bark canoes. Plaintive voices bade farewell over ancestral graves and then as if by signal the high priest of the tribe gave a trumpet blast and with (their) Ark of Covenant held aloft the strange cavalcade of Shawnees coursed southward as mournful strains of music wafted on the spring tide breeze.

Notes

[1] Notice of Josiah Clawson and Martha Russell's marriage can be found on microfilm at the Sidney Ohio Public Library in a listing of early Shelby County marriages. However, Josiah's name was erroneously spelled "Isaiah" in this list. This compilation was drawn from a number of sources including newspapers that are no longer in existence.

[2] Legal records pertaining to Josiah Clawson may be viewed at the Allen County Courthouse in Lima, Ohio. The probate of his estate can be requested for research under the supervision of the Clerk of Court's office as it is in very fragile condition. The probate material contains lists of heirs and persons who purchased goods from the sale of Josiah's estate. These names have potential for important connections in genealogical research in Allen and Putnam Counties.

[3] Allen County, Ohio histories all make mention of the Russells as first occupants of the abandoned Fort Amanda. It is from the research provided by Donald and Janice Russell, Russell family descendents, that we have a firsthand account of early life at the fort.

---

[4] The Russell manuscript and the Russell genealogy materials provided much valuable information for these pages. It is important to note that the Russell genealogy is on file with the Church of the Latter Day Saints library in Salt Lake City, Utah. These files can also be accessed through local CLDS history libraries.

[5] Material on the Hire family was obtained in census reports; land transaction documents, local histories, and above all from the materials that our second cousin Olen Fosnaugh had collected while investigating the Hires for their Revolutionary War ties. The Hire/Clawson military history was submitted by Olen Fosnaugh to the Sons of the American Revolution for his acceptance as a member. One may request background materials from the National Society Sons of the American Revolution, 1000 S. 4th St., Louisville, KY, 40203. A small fee is required for various documents.

[6] Materials on the Hartshorn and DeLong families came primarily from sources in Washington County, Ohio. The staff at the Washington County Historical Society in Marietta provided me with a copy of Edward Hartshorn and Lydia DeLong's marriage certificate, a brief genealogy of the Hartshorn family, and historical references to the Hartshorns and DeLongs from various sources. They also provided directions to the small hamlet of Hartshorn northeast of Marietta and to cemeteries where family members were buried. The Marietta Public Library was helpful in providing historical material on Marietta and material that made mention of our ancestors. The Washington County Courthouse held a valuable piece of information, Jonathan DeLong's will. Records of early Hartshorn land transactions in Marietta were obtained on film from my local CLDS history center. (The college library at Marietta holds original correspondence from Hartshorns in the East directing the Hartshorns already settled in Marietta to purchase various tracts of land.) To obtain George Hartshorn's will, I had to travel to the Jefferson County Courthouse in Steubenville, Ohio, as George had relocated there in his later years. (The Hartshorn book by Derrick S. Hartshorn III contains the full text of George's will on page 619.)

[7] The marriage certificate of Mary Cramer (also called "Polly") and Edward Hartshorn is on file at the Knox County courthouse in Mt. Vernon, Ohio. Also held there are land transactions which bear Edward's name only and purchase of lands bearing both signatures. The 1850 census of Allen County, Ohio, lists Edward Hartshorn children widely ranging in age, leading one to assume that two marriages were involved. Mary is not listed in 1850. However, shortly after their arrival in Allen County in 1834, Edward and Mary engaged in a number of land transactions and those records are held at the Allen County courthouse along with a number of land exchanges attributed to Edward and his son Elmore.

[8] Henry Harvey's *History of the Shawnee* gives a thorough account of Duchoquette's long enduring friendship with the Shawnee and his attempted journey to Washington, D.C., on their behalf.

[9] Burkhardt's front page article entitled "Shawnee Indian Tribe Most Distinctive People of Race" was printed in *The Lima Gazette*, Sunday, March 28, 1926.

Chapter Four: The 1830s Settlers

In September 1836, Attorney Elmore (Elmer) Hartshorn married Casander McHenry, daughter of Reverend Isaac McHenry and Jemima Gaskill. Like the Gaskills, the McHenrys, had come to the Bluffton, Ohio, area from Fayette County, Ohio. The Hartshorn/McHenry union produced five children, one of whom, Malinda Emily, born November 2, 1850, was to become our paternal great-grandmother.

Isaac McHenry was born December 17, 1763 in Hampshire County, Virginia (West Virginia), son of Samuel McHenry.[1] Samuel's father was Barnaby McHenry. Two sons, Isaac and John, were named in Samuel's will. Isaac married Margaret Blair, daughter of William Blair in 1785 in Harrison County, Virginia. Isaac and Margaret came to Kentucky in 1786 where she appears to have died but Isaac stayed on until 1807. Isaac and Margaret were the parents of seven children who were left in his care at her death. Isaac and his children relocated to Fayette County, Ohio, where he married Jemima Gaskill Evertson on November 20, 1815. (Isaac was an ordained Baptist minister and had received a ministerial license in Ross County, Ohio, in 1807.) It is possible that he lived in Ross County before moving to Fayette County. It is also possible that he knew of the Fort Amanda and Fort Jennings area because of his service in the military. Hundreds, perhaps thousands, of men passed this way going up and down the Auglaize River in the War of 1812. Wherever he lived, he attended to the needs of the Baptists throughout a wide area. He lost title to his land in Pickaway County and removed to the area of Bluffton, Ohio, where he was for a time a part of a group of Baptist settlers that included the Gaskills.

By 1830 Isaac and Jemima had relocated to the Auglaize River area becoming neighbors of the Clawsons and Hartshorns. Isaac had served in the Cornstock Militia in 1793 from Green County, Kentucky, and again as an Indian spy in the War of 1812. In 1835 Isaac had the distinction of being the first person to file a petition in the newly formed Putnam County Court. In it he petitioned the federal government for his pension for time he had served in the Revolutionary War. His papers signifying his enlistment had been burned in an Indian raid in Kentucky. Although many persons attested to his story, including Josiah Clawson and Caleb Gaskill, his petition was denied. In 1840 Attorney Elmore Hartshorn, now a family member by marriage, engaged in a land transaction with Isaac and Jemima in Putnam County. This may be the last record of their stay in Ohio as no wills or deaths can be found relating to Isaac and Jemima. It is believed that they moved westward as a result of his ministerial work.

Jemima Gaskill Evertson, a widow, had been married previously to Barnet Evertson and was the mother of three children. She was the daughter of Caleb Gaskill and Hope Russell and was born in New Jersey in 1773 or 1724. Jemima was a sixth-generation American, her family having come in New Jersey in the early seventeenth century. Jemima's great-grandparents were Zacharia Rossell, born in 1692, and Rebecca Lippincott, born 1684. The birthplace of both great-grandparents was North Hampton, Burlington, New Jersey. Her English heritage can be further traced to Sir William Shreve and Lady Jane Fairfax and the birth of their son, William Shreve, in 1592 on the Isle of Wright.

The Kamp Papers written by Gayle O. Kamp in 1986 contains an excellent chronicle of the Gaskill family in America beginning with the first record of the families' progenitor, Edward Gaskoyne in 1636 with a purchase of land in the Town of Salem, Massachusetts Bay. He was a shipwright and came to Salem as an employee of Richard Hollingsworth, who had arrived a year earlier. He and his descendants, who were Quakers, suffered greatly for their beliefs in the succeeding generations. The name Casander appears in the family beginning with the second generation when Edward's son married Provided Southwick, daughter of Lawrence and Casander Southwick, and continued unabated until Casander McHenry's time. The Gaskills were seafarers and fisherman. In time the Gaskills dispersed to other eastern states, some to Pennsylvania, and then eventually Ohio.

Samuel Gaskill, uncle to Jemima and veteran of the Revolutionary War having served as a lieutenant in Stryker's Jerseymen, relocated his family from New Jersey to Pennsylvania. He was accompanied by his brother Caleb, who had also served as a private in Stryker's Jerseymen under Colonel Israel Shreve. Along with a group of Quakers, Colonel Shreve moved to Fayette County, Pennsylvania.

Most of the men in the group had been disowned by the Quakers because of their military service. In 1809 members of the group moved to Ohio, first to Pickaway and then to Fayette County. In 1813 Samuel, his brother Caleb, and his wife Lucretia became charter members of a Baptist Church organized by the Baptist Society in Fayette County, Ohio. It seems only logical that the marriage of Isaac and Jemima came out of this church relationship and this relationship continued with the move of both families to the Auglaize River area.

Notes

[1] Gayle O. Kamp's *The Kamp Papers, Volume II* was invaluable to me in tracing the McHenrys and Gaskills. The full text of Isaac McHenry's pension petition is carried in Kamp's book as well as in Hartshorn's *Hartshorn Families in America.* Jemima's ancestors appear to be the first of our direct lineage to arrive in America and the most documented in England, their homeland. Allen County histories make mention of Isaac's ministerial work, and land documents locate the McHenry home on the Auglaize River astride the Allen/Putnam County lines. Jemima Gaskill Evertson McHenry's genealogy can be found on file with the CLDS.

Chapter Five: The German Catholic Immigrants of the 1840s

In 1844, the same year that Josiah Clawson died, only a few miles to the west, a great deal of excitement was beginning to take place. A whole new community had began to spring up in 1842, at first called Section 10 and then Ten Mile Woods by its Northern German immigrant residents, and later named Delphos[1] by its patron and founder, The Reverend John Otto Bredeick. This year also marked another special event. A roadway was hacked out of the wilderness from the Auglaize River through the Clawson property to this new German village. Among these German settlers who arrived in 1844 and 1845 were the antecedents of the maternal side of our family. These ancestors, however, did not seek the Auglaize River for its commerce and transportation possibilities but instead came to build canals that would become the vehicle of their industry. They were, after all, from the land of canals just below the Holland border.

Reverend Bredeick, the founder of Delphos, Ohio, was the scion of a wealthy mercantilist German family in the German state of Westphalia. For many years, the Catholics of this northernmost German state had been severely prejudiced against and persecuted for their beliefs and found themselves with little opportunities beyond serfdom and hard labor. In Westphalia the Napoleonic Wars had brought to power a repressive anti-Catholic king who stripped Catholic citizens of their rights and their property.

Born to wealth and opportunity, John Otto Bredeick had resolved early in life to help his people. His ultimate solution was to physically remove these poor people from the lands of their overlords to the freedom and open spaces of America.

As Bredeick grew up, the political situation in his German state become almost intolerable and it was feared that a religious revolution was inevitable. The population was angry and crushed into ignorance by a king who denied them access to education, commerce and industry. The Catholics were forced to work as subsistence farmers for wealthy landholders and had little hope, little happiness, and much suffering. Most were unable even to sign their names, much less read a book or buy on the open market. Few were allowed to travel freely, and many were jailed, tortured, or put to death for their faith.

There were, of course, exceptions to the rule, those Catholic families of wealth and power. Some were royals themselves, cousins to the rulers and therefore tolerated as long as they practiced their religion quietly. The king did not dare take their property as he would risk losing advantage of their wealth and skills. Many royals were not qualified to manage such holdings had the lands and businesses been confiscated.

So it was that certain of the families of Germany were able to live their faith quietly and without great difficulty. Among these was the Bredeick family of the city of Verl, Germany. For hundreds of years this family had quietly practiced their religion and often provided sons and daughters to the seminary and convent. The Bredeicks, who maintained close ties to the rulers of both Hanover and France, provided excellent educational opportunities to their children and served as retainers, lawyers and advisors to the royals.

The eldest of seven children, John Otto was born June 23, 1789 to Johann and Maria Bredeick. As the heir to the Bredeick fortune, John Otto was set on a path of classical study, the law and public service. Like many of his contemporaries, his goal was to work for a unified and powerful Germany. But he had another goal of equal importance – to alleviate the suffering of his Catholic countrymen. He was intensely political and well aware of the freedom of religion offered in America. His efforts to work for Catholic religious freedom within the government were to no avail. In 1818, at the age of 29, he left public service and entered the seminary for the diocese of Osnabruck. This was a dream that John Otto had postponed since his youth, hoping that his time in public service would effect the religious tolerance changes he sought.

Because of his family connections, John Otto was allowed considerable freedom while in the seminary and maintained close ties with his family, especially with his brothers Josef Leopold and Ferdinand.

John Otto Bredeick was ordained a priest at Osnabruck in 1822 and rose swiftly up the ecclesiastical ladder becoming Rector of the cathedral parish in 1828. Plans were being made to elevate him even further in the church hierarchy when his brother Ferdinand was arrested for taking part in anti-government activity. Ferdinand had been part of the underground resistance movement since he was a teenager and had been saved many times by his influential brother from punishment for his efforts in stirring up the poor to resist the ruling classes. Using all his political powers and his position as Rector, John Otto was able to negotiate his brother's release, but at a price. Ferdinand would have to leave the kingdom, and indeed, all Germany, to be forever exiled from the land he loved. A considerable bribe to the authorities gave the Bredeick family time to decide a course of action.

The entire Bredeick clan gathered to consider what could be done. It was decided that twenty-six-year-old Ferdinand be sent to America with funds available from John Otto's fortune to find land suitable to re-locate a large number of the German Catholic families from northern German towns and villages. Ferdinand was given explicit instructions, which he took great pains to memorize, a wallet full of cash and extravagant letters of credit. He was put in the care of a priest, Father Johann Hortsman of Glandorf, Germany, whom Reverend Bredeick had previously given permission to establish a settlement in the swamplands of northwest Ohio.

Ferdinand met with Father Hortsman upon arrival in New York and reported to his family that the eastern states were very much like home. He was not, however, favorably impressed with Hortsman's chosen site in Ohio but instead proceeded to Detroit in 1834 and rode horseback west through Indiana, Illinois, Iowa, down into Kansas and Missouri and then back east. He determined at last to purchase lands in western Indiana and Iowa and notified his family of his decisions. That being done, he returned to "new" Glandorf, Father Horstman's settlement, to marry a young lady he had met there on his previous journey.

This was a fateful trip for Ferdinand, for it was in Glandorf that he met Samuel Forrer, a young engineer sent by the State of Ohio to survey and lay out a system of canals in northwest Ohio that would eventually connect Lake Erie to the Ohio River. Forrer proposed three possible routes for the canal system, one to follow the flow of the Auglaize River and two cutting through the flat lands and the swamps. Forrer's enthusiasm about the canals' role in the future development of Ohio was contagious. Based on his new friendship with Forrer and believing in the possibilities that the canal system would bring to northwest Ohio, Ferdinand advised his German family that he had made a new choice.

This kind of development was most exciting to Ferdinand, as the Germans in northern Germany were masters of canal building and could readily see the potential for settlement, commerce and industry along its banks. In a practice that would be frowned upon today, advising the Bredeick family members and a political friend, William Webb, who would later become Governor of Ohio, Forrer quickly bought up numerous parcels of land along all three proposed routes. Banking on the choice of the canal following the Auglaize River, Ferdinand bought extensive land at Fort Jennings and took up residence there with his new family near the old 1812 fort. After the State of Ohio chose one of the non-river routes for the canal construction, Forrer made another bold move. Again not to be outdone, Forrer bid to become the primary construction engineer for the Miami Extension Canal to run from present-day St. Marys, Ohio to Defiance, Ohio.

Fortunately, Ferdinand had purchased a number of parcels of land that became the ideal site for a new community where there was generous wide water and a millpond. These conditions suggested construction of dry and wet docks, boat yard, mills and other water related businesses. Boat builders were recruited from the Lake Erie area to construct the canal boats. In three years they constructed eighteen vessels.

Meanwhile, back in Germany John Otto chafed to be away from his clerical duties and spent the years until 1844 attempting to convince the superior of his diocese to release him for foreign duty. Had he not been held in such esteem, his release would have been accomplished much more easily, but because of John Otto's wealth and family connections the Church was extremely reluctant to let such a rising star go, especially to an unknown fate in a faraway land. Ferdinand's brother-in-law, Theodore Wrocklage, traveled to Germany to make a presentation directly to the Bredeick family and to the Bishop.

As a result John Otto was given permission to put together a group to sail to America in 1842; however, the Bishop rescinded his pledge to let John Otto accompany them. This mission was financed by John Otto and his brother Joseph. The people who chose to go were penniless peasants and serfs who were uneducated, untrained, and completely dependent on Theodore Wrocklage, their guide and protector. Many volunteers backed out when they learned that John Otto would not accompany them. Just forty-two persons made this first voyage to their new homeland. On board the ship were the supplies they would need to start their lives in the settlement, Ten Mile Woods, the beginnings of which were being built around the new canal system.

These settlers arrived first by ship to New York, and then traveled across New York State to Buffalo on the Erie Canal. From Buffalo they traveled by lake to Toledo, Ohio, and then by canal again to Defiance, Ohio. These hearty Germans were impressed with the new canal waterways and their eventual importance to the development of their new home. From Defiance they traveled overland by wagon and on foot through dense forests over the Defiance Trail, which followed the Auglaize River. It would have not been uncommon for them to have encountered the wild animals that still inhabited the area of northwest Ohio. Among those would have been wolves, bears and puma. They arrived safely at their final destination on November 1, 1843.

The settlement that they reached must have been a great shock to them after hearing the glowing reports of Wrocklage and Reverend Bredeick. Only a few rude structures existed, occupied by persons who had moved to the Ten Mile Woods from Fort Jennings and Glandorf Piles of mud and great gaping holes in the earth around the canal construction dominated the site. The first night the exhausted immigrants slept in their wagons. By the next morning these hearty folk were up and ready to pitch in to "conquer" the swamps and forests they had encountered along the way. None had funds, so they took no-interest, long-term loans from the Bredeicks for large one- and two-dollar-an-acre tracts of land outside the settlement. They had no education or training to be shopkeepers or other mercantilists. What they were qualified to be were farmers – men who, for the first time in their lives, would own the land they farmed. Anticipating this, John Otto ordered that "Americans" be enticed to the settlement to begin building the businesses and services that this growing community would need.

The winter of 1834 was unusually harsh, and as a result most of the inhabitants moved to cabins already erected on the Auglaize River. For the first time these "late comers" became temporary neighbors to those like the Clawsons and Hartshorns who had already taken up residence along the river. In the spring the Germans moved back to Ten Mile Woods to begin building the settlement in earnest. The immigrants were soon joined by Americans who had been given free lots on which to construct their stores and shops. It was Reverend Bredeick's wish that his new town grow and prosper rapidly, and he had no wish that the community would become a national enclave for Germans seeking to build "a new Germany." Every effort was made to attract men of ability and education and men who had influential contacts.

Reverend Bredeick finally received permission to come to America in 1844, and this time the group sailed under his direction and protection. Sailing with Bredeick on this 1844 voyage were all the persons who would become our maternal ancestors. When Bredeick arrived at his settlement in October 1844, he faced the reality that the immigrants who preceded him had not done well without his leadership. Only a humble gathering of huts and cabins greeted him. His dreams of an eventual metropolis of a million people at the hub of a thriving canal system must have seemed far away indeed.

Surveying the needs of the little community, Reverend Bredeick quickly called a meeting of all the inhabitants. In this meeting he laid out the ground rules for setting the community on the right course. Among his pronouncements were that he would immediately assume management of the canal lock operations, that his large cabin would serve as a church until a community building could be built, that he would plot his property into a city, and, most revolutionary of all, that the following morning all residents were to begin formal schooling until each could read and write. Probably most shocking of all the pronouncements to the German immigrants was that Reverend Bredeick had set aside land not only for a Catholic church but also for Lutheran, Methodist, and Presbyterian churches in their community. What Bredeick was personally promising to his new community was a literate society and religious freedom, a concept as alien as ownership of land had been in the old country. One can imagine the wonderment these humble peasants must have experienced at hearing their leader's vision. Reverend Bredeick pledged that never again would religious hatred be allowed to oppress anyone – at least not in this new community which he had re-named Delphos.

However, the near result of Bredeick's pronouncements was to drive these new Americans back to the land. Some had dreamt of becoming merchants, shopkeepers, and integral members to the new community. This was not to be in the beginning; their lot was either to till the land or work by the day on the canal system. Bredeick put the word out far and wide that he would give choice lots on the canal frontage to manufacturers, financiers, bankers, mercantilists and other professionals who would join his new "plantation."

The German immigrants had left the oppression of the old world behind; the effect of all these rulings and preferences was to cause almost immediate resentment. When Bredeick announced that he would build a very large church in the center of the settlement, resentment boiled over. They felt that this was inappropriate to the new world as it would be a symbol of what they had left behind in their home. As the new church, huge in its proportions, began to take shape, many citizens traveled miles out of their way to attend small and humble churches that they felt more befitting their new status as Americans.

As the canal system was being completed, its builders sensed the importance of rail travel which was inching its way across the country. John Otto, always alert to emerging trends, began to plan for and lobby for Delphos to become an important rail center. To achieve this goal he did two important things. He managed to push through the Ohio Legislature a charter for the City of Delphos in February 1851, and he donated heavily to those groups in the East who were to determine which westward cities would become railway centers. All was in place for Delphos as a strong contender in 1854 when disaster struck the little city: a cholera epidemic broke out and was so devastating that by 1855 Delphos had lost half its population. The railroad authorities, fearing sending workers into the area, crossed Delphos off their list. Delphos would later have access to cross-country passenger and freight service, but it never became a rail center of the proportions John Otto had hoped. Samuel Forrer, always the transportation visionary, advised Reverend Bredeick to concentrate on roadways as the key to the future. In this speculation Forrer proved to be correct as the canals were quickly usurped by the railroads and, in turn, the railroads' functions would in time be given over to highway travel and transport.

Ferdinand Bredeick had died in 1846 leaving his older brother grief-stricken. When the rail center possibility fell through, Reverend Bredeick was further saddened and his health began to decline. John Hertz, his friend and the planner/builder of the wooden church, died in the cholera epidemic, leaving the construction project for others to finish. A greatly weakened Reverend Bredeick addressed his congregation in the imposing drafty church structure on Easter Sunday 1858. In his remarks he urged his flock to move forward in building the community they had all envisioned when they arrived at Ten Mile Woods. Father John Otto Bredeick died August 21, 1858, his dreams of a great utopia in Middle America unfulfilled.

Reverend Bredeick made generous bequests to both Delphos and nearby Ottoville, where he had also founded a new congregation. To both he left the funds to build magnificent new Catholic facilities, some of which stand today as a monument to his vision. It is believed that St. John's Catholic Church in Delphos is the largest non-cathedral church in America. Throughout his years in Ohio, John Otto had also contributed large sums of money to help the oppressed Catholics in northern Germany that he had reluctantly left behind.

Late nineteenth-century engraving of St. John the Evangelist Catholic
Church, Delphos, Ohio.

After the cholera epidemic, many of the farm folk moved into Delphos and took over the businesses and shops vacated by the non-German Americans who had lost their lives. These men and women were no longer the uneducated serfs and peasants who left their homeland to follow the plan laid out for them by their trusted mentor, John Otto. They were now literate landholders and capable independent farmers. Perhaps, after all, they were the instruments of the fulfillment of Reverend Bredeick's dreams.

Delphos never became the shining city of a million souls that John Otto envisioned. Instead, it became a typical small Midwestern town, the center of commerce and society for a portion of northwest Ohio and a refuge to those who prefer the pace and closeness of small town life. All around its edges are the large farms where the surnames of those who came to Ten Mile Woods so long ago are repeated through the generations. Among those acreages are the farms of our maternal ancestors who all came to America from a village in Northern Germany called Melle under Reverend Bredeick's care.

Notes

[1] Background information concerning the formation and settlement of Delphos, Ohio, was drawn from Allen and Van Wert County histories, articles in the local paper *The Delphos Herald*, and the book *Reflections 1812-1960*. The principle sources, however, were three publications: *Delphos Vicenqui – Bicentennial History Book*, *The Centenary of St. John the Baptist Church, Delphos, Ohio, 1881-1981*, *Reverend John Bredeick, A Bicentennial Perspective, January 23, 1789-January 23, 1989*, and *Samuel Forrer Absentee Landlord*. Inquiries concerning these publications may be directed to the Delphos Chamber of Commerce, the Delphos Public library and the Delphos Canal Commission.

Chapter Six: The Lause/Pohlman Connection

With the approval of his release from his German duties, Reverend Bredeick soon set in motion events that would impact our ancestry and further bring together the elements of our heritage.

View of original home of Lause family in Wellingholzhausen, Germany, taken in 1990.

Detail of Lause home with inscription above entrance taken in 1990.

Two of our paternal great-grandparents came to America on the ship *Isabella* with Reverend Bredeick in 1844. On board the *Isabella* were the families of Henry "Joseph Henry" Lause and Casper Pohlman.[1] Henry Lause and his wife Elizabeth Giesker were accompanied by their five children, one of whom was a twenty year old named Frederick. Six children, one of whom was Mary (then just six years old), accompanied Casper Pohlman and his wife Clara Maria Henseler. Nine years later, Mary would become the wife of Frederick Lause and would become in time our maternal great-grandmother. Frederick's father Henry was born in Wellingholthausen, Germany in 1791, and his wife Mary Elizabeth in Melle, Germany in 1793. Casper Pohlman was born about 1803 in Wellingholthausen. His wife Clara Maria was born in the Hanover area about 1810.

Wellingholzhausen street scene taken in 2002.

View of St. Bartholomaus Catholic Church in Wellingholzhausen, Germany.
Thought to be home church of Lause family.

Frederick, who was born in Melle, Germany, in March 1825, was an apprentice to Casper Pohlman in the art of cabinetmaking. Mary Pohlman was born to Casper and Maria in August of 1838 in Melle. Frederick continued as an apprentice cabinetmaker and then farmer upon arriving in America. Frederick and Casper formed a lifelong partnership and built many homes and other structures in the Delphos area. One can only imagine the developing romance of the apprentice and his master's child as the years passed and Mary grew into womanhood. Their marriage, which took place April 3, 1856, was a long and fruitful one, and together they reared ten children on their well-kept farm just a mile outside the center of Delphos. The Delphos Ohio Canal Museum contains a beautiful piece of Frederick's cabinetry on which he carved a loving dedication to his wife, Mary.

Cabinet built and carved by Frederick Lause II to honor his wife, Mary.
Cabinet is in the collection of the Delphos, Ohio Canal Museum.

Both are buried in the cemetery of St. John's Catholic Church in
Delphos. Mary was well thought of in the community at large. In her
obituary in *The Delphos Herald*, she was praised for the role she had

played in the settlement of Delphos. She was described as a woman with "a retiring disposition, [who] was kind and always had the welfare of her family at heart...."

Frederick and Mary's home exists today much as it did in their lifetimes.

Located a short distance from Delphos, Ohio, and just off of State Road 66, the Frederick Lause, Sr. home continues to serve the Lause family.

The barn, which rests to the right of the house, is a working barn and like
the house remains as a testament to high-quality construction.

When their son Frederick II married Lena Moreo from nearby
Landeck in 1900, it was logical that they, too, would purchase
property near the senior Frederick's farm. Frederick II built, much as
his father had, a large and sturdy house, large red barn, and many
outbuildings. A deep drilled well provided the water for the family
and the animals. Even as a child, I was impressed with the
spaciousness of the house. Everything was over-sized. A huge kitchen
and dining room, living room, parlor and bedroom occupied the
downstairs. Upstairs there seemed to be no end to spacious bedrooms.
All floors in the house were hardwood, polished to a high sheen.

Under the house was a full basement that contained not only the
furnace and the coal to feed it but huge bins for potatoes and onions
and many shelves for holding the thousand cans of fruit, vegetables,
and meats that my grandmother preserved for consumption
throughout the year. Except for sugar, flour and coffee, the Lause
family was almost totally self-sufficient. The task of providing three

59

meals a day for thirteen people or more must have been daunting – and was surely made even more daunting by the fact that all water had to be carried from the well outside. Electricity came to the Lause home in the early 1930s, but indoor plumbing did not appear until the 1940s. One can only imagine the complications of cooking, cleaning, bathing, and laundry for such a large family. All the water had to be heated on a wood stove in the kitchen before central heating was installed. Light was provided for nighttime activities by kerosene lamps and Coleman lanterns before the arrival of electricity.

The barn, too, was huge with places for the cows, horses, and pigs, and storage of farm equipment and the grains needed to feed the cattle. In addition there were other equipment storage buildings and a smokehouse for preserving meats by smoking. Unfortunately, this welcoming and accommodating house and barn burned to the ground in the 1980s. However, a few photos of the house remain that tell something of its size and construction. Only one equipment structure stands today to mark the home farm of our maternal grandparents and the birthplace of our mother, Viola.

Our maternal grandmother Lena Moreo was born December 29, 1875 in Landeck, Ohio, to Andrew Moreo and Christina Caroline Loy. Her father Andrew Moreo was born in Bavaria in 1844. Her mother Christina was born in Van Wert, Ohio, in 1857. Christina was the second wife of Andrew, a widower, and father of five children. Andrew and Christina Loy married on August 23, 1877. Andrew and Christina together added six more children to the Moreo brood. Christina's parents were John Loy I, born in Germany, and Sophia Schnieder, born in Ohio. Nothing is known of Andrew's parentage in Germany.

The Andrew Moreo home near the village of Landeck no longer exists, but Andrew and Christina's home in Delphos on Clay Street looks much as it did when Andrew sold his farm shortly before 1917 and the couple moved into Delphos.

This charming little house on Clay Street in Delphos, Ohio, remains much as it was when the Moreo family occupied it in the early twentieth century.

In 1916 Christina had a stroke which left her paralyzed on the left side of her body, and in a wheelchair for the rest of her life. Our mother Viola, daughter of Frederick II, remembers Christina well and speaks of her with great admiration. Despite being paralyzed, she continued to do all her own housework and childrearing from her wheelchair and managed to express herself through body language and through one short phrase that she could speak, "No wonder." Christina died in 1936, and Andrew just a year later. Both are buried in the St. John's Catholic cemetery in Delphos.

Wedding portrait of Lena Moreo and Frederick Lause II.

When Helena "Lena" Moreo, daughter of Andrew Moreo and Christina Loy, married Frederick Lause II on October 24, 1900, in a Catholic ceremony in St. John's church, her expectations of her future were probably well-based on the near past and the experiences of the farm wives who had emigrated from Germany to the Delphos area more than a half-century earlier. The farm on State Road 66 where she and her husband chose to build their life together was just two miles from the heart of the Catholic community in Delphos. The farm was small, just a little more than forty acres, but the young couple, hard-working and of peasant stock, were confident in their ability to build a good life for themselves and their future children on this property. Families were very large in those early days of the 20th century, as help was needed to manage these small farms well, and a growing family, too, would have been the natural expectation of the newlyweds. Twelve children were born to Lena and Frederick. Eleven reached adulthood. Our mother Viola was born the fourth child, and the second of three girls, on February 4, 1909.

Notes

[1] The material in this chapter comes from a variety of sources: county histories, family stories, the national census, and personal observation. The most significant sources used, however, are those recorded and held by St. John's Catholic Church in Delphos, Ohio. This was, after all, a community founded by a Catholic priest for the German émigrés under his care. In its beginning years every aspect of the settlement of Delphos, to one degree or another, was connected to the Church. For this the genealogist can be thankful. As an example, it took me ten years to finally discover the name of the ship that the Kunzes traveled on to America but only a very short time to locate the ship's name that carried the Lause ancestors to their new settlement. St. John's genealogical records have now been computerized providing even more ready assistance to the researcher.

Chapter Seven: Along the Auglaize in the 1850s

Life along the Auglaize River in the little community of Delphos and the other small surrounding communities settled in comfortably in the years between the departure of the last Indian peoples in the 1840s and the onset of the Civil War. Swamps were drained, fertile farms developed, canal travel and then rail travel came into its own, and a network of improved roadways and bridges were constructed. Substantial courthouses and city halls were built, and public schools, libraries, and churches were established throughout the countryside. In addition, another kind of "railway" was being promoted in the Ohio country as early as the 1830s as anti-slavery citizens risked great danger to their lives bringing African American slaves north across the Ohio River from the slave state, Kentucky.[1]

One can only imagine the excitement of these early Ohio immigrants as they began to learn how to read and write and the pleasure they found in being in charge of their own destinies. Many who had so recently been serfs or peasants were now prosperous farmers, merchants, and manufacturers. Families like the Hartshorns who had not so recently come from abroad enhanced their education and became doctors, engineers, lawyers, nurses, and other professionals. All were focused on becoming a valuable and integral part of this new country they were helping to build. They no longer had to take second place to the "Americans." They *were* the Americans.

Josiah Clawson, Jr., answered the call of the Union Army on August 22, 1862, to the 118th Ohio Volunteer Infantry.[2] He served in numerous battles throughout the war and was dismissed on June 14, 1865. Three other Clawson young men from Allen County served in the Civil War. Hiram, who was also in the 118th O.V.I., had enlisted a month before Josiah and was killed in March 1864. Josiah's regiment participated in thirteen significant battles of the Civil War in Georgia, Tennessee, and North Carolina, including the siege of Atlanta (see Appendix A). When Josiah Clawson, Jr., died in December 1922, he was honored in his obituaries and at his funeral as an outstanding soldier and citizen. Large flags of The United States of America were draped over his casket at the Methodist Church ceremony and over the hearse which bore his casket to the Walnut Grove Cemetery a few miles east of Delphos. Malinda, his wife of 54 years and mother of his twelve children, had preceded him in death three years earlier.

Malinda, daughter of Elmore Hartshorn and Casander McHenry, was just sixteen when she married Josiah Clawson, Jr., on March 3, 1866. Although the Hartshorn, Clawson, McHenry and other aforementioned families were the earliest settlers on the Auglaize River and often quite close neighbors, marrying the seasoned war veteran six years her senior must have been quite a giant step for such a young woman who had known nothing but that small stretch of riverfront.

Malinda Hartshorn portrait taken after the close of the Civil War. Portrait may have been taken on the occasion of her engagement or wedding to Josiah.

Josiah Clawson portrait taken after the close of the Civil War. Portrait may have been taken on the occasion of his engagement or wedding to Malinda.

Doubtless Josiah had known Malinda since she was a child. They were married at the Clawson homestead, where they spent the early part of their marriage before moving further downstream on the Auglaize and establishing their own farm. Their small frame farmhouse still exists and is in use today. Josiah and Malinda retired from farming in 1914 and moved to Delphos to their new home at the corner of Douglas and 3rd Streets.

Portrait taken of Josiah Jr. and Malinda Clawson on their fiftieth wedding anniversary.

Malinda, a pretty girl at sixteen, remained quite attractive during her lifetime. Her life could not have been an easy one. She bore twelve children of whom three died in infancy and a son, Roy, died seven weeks before her death. I knew of her only through my great aunts and uncles and my paternal grandmother Deflora as Malinda had died when my father was just a boy. Nonetheless, even as a child it was apparent to me that Malinda's and Josiah's children had been reared with kindness and love. Through them, I had my first sense of my British Hartshorn ancestors. The great-aunts and great-uncles that I was privileged to spend a little time with as a very young person were intelligent and kind, possessed of elegant good manners and a great sense of adventure. When my great-aunts gathered for any small occasion one could expect a full-fledged tea party with hours of gentle conversation and small dishes of all sorts of foods brought out of cupboards and iceboxes. Even as a small child I decided that these women were on to something. This was fun and definitely something I would like to do "when I grew up."

Except for the daughter Monna, Malinda's and Josiah's adult children all married, had children, and stayed in the Delphos-Lima area. Monna married Glen Fosnaugh, a young man from nearby Van Wert who was a farmer with his eyes set on the West. When their firstborn Olen was a small boy in the early 1900s, the Fosnaughs decided to pioneer in western Canada. They sold their farm and packed up their personal belongings, household furnishings, farm equipment, and animals, and set out in railroad boxcars for Alberta, Canada. Monna recalled later that when they reached Chicago they sat on a railroad siding for six weeks waiting for a rail connection.

When they finally arrived at Calgary, Alberta, they headed by rail again, this time north toward Edmonton. Along the way the train stopped at a tiny settlement called LaCombe. Standing by the rail siding was a large group of early settlers who urged them to go no further but stay and claim their land there. The Fosnaughs heeded their advice and claimed several hundred acres of farmland from which one can see far to the west the Banff Mountains. This was Cree Indian country and many Cree Indians continued to live on their farm in their own fragile dwellings. Many times Monna and Glen took in the Indian families in the bitter Alberta winters. Monna also was always at hand when an Indian baby was born and assisted with many of the children's births. Theirs was a life of peaceful co-existence. A second son, Robert, was born to the Fosnaughs after their arrival in Canada and has remained there with his family on his deceased parents' original land holdings.

The Fosnaughs never gave up their American citizenship but remained dual citizens. Olen, the eldest son, became a tree geneticist and lived out his adult life across the border in Washington where he was employed as the official tree forester for the state. Olen wrote a book on tree genetics as a result of his academic studies that remains to this day a definitive treatise on tree genetics. After Olen's retirement from his state position, the State of Washington flew him in an "air boxcar" to Germany each year to select trees for planting in Washington.

I had the pleasure of visiting with Monna and Glen Fosnaugh in 1969. Glen was still keeping bees and tinkering in his blacksmith's shop. Monna was busy with the farm chores and keeping the log house that they had built together so many years ago. Glen's favorite thing to do in his retirement was to go shopping in nearby Red Deer. I shall never forget the day we went looking for an IBM Selectric typewriter and a stereo, two items high on his shopping list. Glen "dressed" for the occasion: blue denim coveralls, denim shirt, and red bandana around his neck.

I soon learned the purpose for the "country finery." We would go into a shop selling these items and the clerk would immediately take him for a country rube. The clerk would offer him the cheapest stereo or typewriter, believing that would be all he could afford or have the capability of using. Glen, with a devilish gleam in his eyes, would play his game with them insisting, "No, no, that's not what I want," until they were completely baffled and exasperated, clearly just wanting to get rid of this stubborn and eccentric old man. At a moment when the clerk was completely out of patience, Glen would point to the most expensive typewriter or stereo in the store, and softly announce, "I'll take that." And so saying, he would pull out of his back pocket a roll of bills almost three inches, thick leaving the clerk greatly taken aback.

Having had his day of great fun with these "newcomers," Glen loaded up his new stereo and typewriter in his battered old truck and we set out to find an "ice cream parlor" where we would celebrate his little victories. I often wondered whether he ever used either appliance after I returned to Ohio or if he had just told and retold, with great relish, to all who would listen the story of his big shopping day in Red Deer with his young cousin from "The States." However, be that as it may, I treasure to this day a little English bone china dish that he bought for me after we finished our ice cream, a souvenir of our day in Red Deer.

Unfortunately, many of us lost our grandparents when we were young or were caught up in building our own lives that it never occurred to us to ask the really important questions about them. Questions about their backgrounds, their hopes and dreams, a touching simple question such as, "How did you meet?" As a consequence, when we begin finally to research our backgrounds, we have only dry bits of paper and our brief memories and old photos to imagine the answers to our queries. How I wish I could have asked that question of all our grandparents. In most cases our ancestors met through neighborhood proximity or a church both held in common. In the case of our maternal grandparents, Lena Moreo and Frederick Lause II, it may have been both proximity and shared religion. Both families had farms close to each other near Landeck, Ohio, and doubtless both families attended the Catholic church in that small village.

With our fraternal grandparents, Deflora Clawson (daughter of Josiah and Malinda Clawson) and Ferdinand (son of Franz Michael and Margaretha Kunz, it was neither. Deflora grew up near the Auglaize River on the Defiance Trail east of Delphos, and Ferdinand was reared several miles west of Delphos on McKibben Road. Deflora was Methodist and Ferdinand Catholic. By further contrast, Deflora could have traced most of her ancestors in America to the eighteenth century or earlier. Ferdinand's parents, Franz Michael Kunz and his wife Margaretha Martz, arrived in America in 1854 with four children born in their hometown of Rheinzabern, Germany. Ferdinand was born in Dayton, Ohio, six years after their arrival. The Kunz family moved from Montgomery County to Allen County after Ferdinand's birth. The Clawsons and Kunzes came from vastly different cultural areas of Europe: the former from the flatlands and canals of Holland and the south of England while the Kunzes were solidly planted for many generations in the central southern Rheinlands. Yet the two families had many things in common. Ferdinand's father was a craftsman, builder, and farmer, as were many of Deflora's ancestors, and both families were highly adventurous and open to change.

It appears that when Franz Michael Kunz and his wife Margaretha and their four children arrived in New York on the ship *Lisbon* in May 1854, they arranged for travel directly to Dayton in central Ohio.[3] It is not known why their destination was Dayton except to say that a number of Martz families had emigrated to Dayton from Germany and Pennsylvania in the mid-nineteenth century. It is possible that there was a familial connection to Dayton through Margaretha. Exhaustive research in the Dayton area has produced very few Kunzes in residence at that time, and none has been proven to be related to Franz Michael. A second cousin, who now lives in San Antonio, Texas, recalls that her family believed that the

Congregationalist Church had brought the Kunzes to America. Again, no documentation is presently available that would substantiate that.

The captain of the *Lisbon*, which departed from the port of Le Havre, France, listed 354 passengers when the ship arrived in New York and further noted that all who left France were in good health upon arrival. All adult males were identified as being farmers. These scanty details led this researcher on a merry chase for twenty years, until only a few months ago when, with the help of a German researcher, I finally found the documents attesting to the births of Franz Michael and Margaretha, their marriage, the birth certificates of the four children born in Germany, the identify of the parents of Franz Michael and Margaretha, and the resignation date of Franz Michael from the Bavarian army in which he had served for six years. It is not known with certainty if the Kunzes were Catholics in Germany as the children, especially the older children, chose other faiths in America. Our great-grandparents were Catholic while living in Allen County, as were the younger children, but the sons and daughter born in Germany chose to join other denominations when they reached adulthood and became quite prominent in their churches.

Franz Michael Kunz was born May 22, 1819, to Franz Anton Kunz and Margaretha Feinholz in Rheinzabern and registered at the County of Candel, Court of Germersheim, District of Rhine, Kingdom of Bavaria. His father was declared to be thirty-three years of age and a farmer by occupation. Witnesses Franz Michael Thomas and Andreas Tentschler, both day workers, attested to his birth. Franz Anton Kunz declared that he could not write and signed with a mark.

Margaretha Martz was born to Franz Michael Martz and Maria Anna Himmelsbach on April 3, 1819, in Rheinzabern and registered in the same county as Franz Michael Kunz, which is noted above. Her father, age 41, declared that he was a farmer. The witnesses to Margaretha's birth were Phillip Jacob Reib, a farmer, and Anton Geldman, a locksmith. The document was signed by Marz, Geldman, Reib, and Officer Topper.

Rheinzabern is located about twenty miles north and a little west of the city of Karlsruhle. The former Roman settlement well-known for its pottery and brick-making appears to have been quite small at the time of Franz Michael and Margaretha's births.

Rheinzabern, Germany, main street scene. Photo taken 2002.

Rheinzabern, Germany, street scene with St. Michael's Catholic Church in
background. Photo taken 2002.

Today pictures of Rheinzabern make it appear very much like a small Midwestern American town with the church being the central architectural feature of the life of the city – a fact that is in keeping with most American immigrants' settlements as they ultimately chose to settle in areas that reminded them greatly of their European homes and set about almost immediately to replicate home and church styles they had left behind. We children of immigrants continue this practice to this day. When I lived in an adobe house in Santa Fe, New Mexico, I surrounded it with a white picket fence and a lawn and flowers. Now that I live again in the Midwest, I have decorated my home with Indian and Spanish weavings and pottery and plant pink and white hollyhocks that remind me of Santa Fe. So it is not surprising that when one visits one's homeland one does feel immediately "at home."

Roman pot found at the site of Rheinzabern. Photo courtesy City of Rheinzabern.

Franz Michael Kunz and Margaretha Martz's marriage certificate contains a wealth of information about both families.[4] They were married May 10, 1847 by the mayor of Rheinzabern, Johann Adam Orth. Margaretha's father was in attendance and "willing with the wedding." Franz Michaels's grandparents are listed with their dates of death; both had passed away prior to 1834. Margaretha's grandparents are not listed but her mother, Maria Anna Himmelsbach, is listed with her date of death as 1829. Franz Michael declared that he was a day worker and that he resided in County Candel, Department of Landau in *der Pfalz*, Kingdom of Bavaria. The groom further declared that he resigned from the military on March 11, 1847, as a member of the Royal Bavarian Infantry Regiment "Herzog Wilhelm" and that he had sworn his oath of citizenship in Rheinzabern. Margaretha is listed as having "no occupation." It is not readily apparent from this civil ceremony that either Franz Michael or Margaretha were practicing Catholics at that time, as to get married only in a civil ceremony would have been unthinkable and prohibited by the Catholic Church. (It should be noted that practicing Catholics were required to have both a civil and a Catholic marriage ceremony.)

Four children were born to Franz Michael and Margaretha in Rheinzabern and all the births are registered there. On each of the registrations Franz Michael is listed as a day worker and Margaretha continues to be listed as "having no occupation." A son, Georg (George) Anton was born to the couple on September 16, 1849; Joseph was born March 2, 1848; Elizabetha on May 12, 1850; and Barbara, April 4, 1853. Barbara was listed as being nine months old on the ship's list and that may have been based on the sailing date rather than on the date of arrival in New York. It was noted on each child's birth certificate that Franz Michael and the witnesses had all signed their own names. It appears that this generation was no longer illiterate; in fact, the will and other legal papers that Franz Michael penned in Ohio bore indications of a very literate man.

By 1860 the Kunz family had settled in comfortably in their new home in Harrison Township in Montgomery County, Ohio. On the 1860 census, Franz (now calling himself Frank) was listed as a gardener with his total assets more than $1,000. During their Dayton years, three more children were born to the Kunz family to join the four children born in Bavaria. Ferdinand, our grandfather, was born in

1860. Franz Michael officially became an American citizen[5] when he renounced his loyalty to the King of Bavaria on September 24, 1859, in Dayton, Ohio.

Children of Franz Michael Kunz taken in early twentieth century at the family home. Left to right seated are Philabena and Elizabeth; standing are Ferdinand, Frank, Joseph, and George Anthony.

Little evidence of Dayton's beginnings would have greeted the mid-nineteenth century immigrant to the area.[6] The settlement of Dayton was originally founded just seventeen days after the signing of the Greenville Treaty. Some of its earliest inhabitants had been residents of Covalt Station and the Fort Washington area. An attempt in 1789 to form a settlement called Venice led by Major Benjamin Sites at this location was abandoned. Indian problems and John Cleve Symmes's differences with Congress contributed to this failed venture. But in August of 1795 a party under the leadership of General Arthur St. Clair, Governor of the Northwest Territory, purchased from Symmes the seventh and eighth ranges between the Mad and Little Miami Rivers, and surveyors were employed to survey the land and mark out a road. The settlement was named Dayton after one of its principal investors, General Jonathan Dayton. Three parties consisting of nineteen men and seventeen women and children left Cincinnati in March of 1796 traveling by water and land through the wilderness to their new home. Several members of Symmes family were amongst the early inhabitants. It is clear that Dayton's settlement was firmly rooted to the major personalities who had come to the Cincinnati area in the late eighteenth century. In less than sixty years this small settlement had grown to the sophisticated city that greeted Margaretha and Franz Michael and their four children.

When the Kunz family arrived in Dayton they were probably pleased to find a thriving and bustling city of over 15,000. Building, development, and expansion were in evidence throughout the city. Travel was facilitated on improved roads and canals, and railroads of varying distances were beginning to be built. (In 1839 Samuel Forrer, who later was so influential in building the canal system in northern Ohio, had been hired by the City of Dayton as its chief engineer in charge of roadways and turnpikes.) Just the year before the Kunz family's arrival, the city had sanctioned a system of public schools and been host to the Ohio State Fair. Beautiful and substantial churches of many denominations greeted the newcomers. Although only a decade separates the Kunz's arrival in Dayton with that of the German immigrants from Melle in northwest Ohio, the contrast in living conditions was dramatic, as was the contrast in work opportunities. In Germany Franz Michael had been a soldier and a farmer; in America he became a gardener, as did his two eldest sons. It is almost certain, however, that he was also a carpenter. When he and his family removed to the Delphos, Ohio, area in the mid 1860s, he built his own home, barn, and other outbuildings which remain today as a testament to his skill. And this skill he passed on to his son Ferdinand, who in turn passed the talent on to his own son Frederick, our father.

The original Kunz home and its outbuildings built on Kiggins Road, a short distance from Delphos, Ohio, continues to be a thriving farm homestead.

The 1882 History of Montgomery County contains written sketches of two of the Kunz children, George and Joseph. Franz Michael is mentioned as their father and as having spent six years in the German army before immigrating to America. Both sons are listed as gardeners. By that date George had married Margorie Bentley, was the father of two small children, and had been influential in building the program at the First Lutheran Church of Dayton. He also helped establish the Patterson Chapel Sabbath School and was its treasurer. But George was not long contented with Dayton. He had his eyes firmly fixed on the West.

The George Anthony Kunz family in an Arkansas portrait.
First row (left to right): Margaret Bentley Kunz, Jeanette, Gladys and
George Anthony Kunz. Second row (left to right): Sara, Clifford Harrison
and Eliza. Top row (left to right): Edwin, Lucy and Elmer.

In the late nineteenth century, George rode on horseback with a
friend to Kansas and Oklahoma, leaving his family behind. In the land
rush in Oklahoma he claimed a piece of land for a homestead.
However, while George returned to Dayton to secure his family for
the move, his claim was usurped. Not one to be daunted by this turn
of events, he again traveled by horseback to Kansas where he settled
his family for a time. A son, Clifford, was born in Kansas. In time the
family again relocated, moving first to Bentonville and then
Fayetteville, Arkansas. It was in Fayetteville that George Anton made
his mark.

In Fayetteville, George became the chief horticulturist for the
University of Arkansas. He maintained large greenhouses for the
university throughout his entire career there. As a result of his
experiences at the university, he wrote a lengthy article for the
university magazine entitled, "How I made Something Magnificent

with My Two Acres."[7] George died August 13, 1930, and is buried in Fayetteville.

The Arkansas Kunz family grew to nine in number and the children for the most part graduated from the university. The older children, who were among the earliest University of Arkansas graduates, were honored by having their names carved into the steps of the old administration building. These steps can still be found on the grounds of University.

Although not all as adventurous as their brother George, the siblings who reached adulthood enjoyed good health and lived out their lives contributing to their families, completing creative endeavors, and continuing involvement in their chosen churches. In the pedigree chart which follows this narrative details are given of each of their lives in depth insofar as they are known at this printing. Below are brief biographies of each.

Joseph Kunz chose not to join his extended family when they moved to the Delphos area.

Portrait of Joseph Kunz as young man taken in Dayton, Ohio.

Joseph married Sarah E. Armstrong in Dayton on May 4, 1871. He and Sarah had five children, one of whom, a little girl, died in childhood. He became the principal gardener for the Dayton State Hospital and attended to many private gardens as well. When he retired from the hospital, he was given many honors for the work he had done in maintaining the grounds during his career. He was a member of the United Brethren Church and is buried in the old Greencastle Cemetery in Dayton.

Elizabeth also remained in Dayton and married Henry Michael Hager. Their son Frank, born June 1, 1878, became a professor of languages and taught at a number of Midwestern universities. Frank Hager attended the 1936 Olympics in Germany and while there researched Elizabeth's genealogy. To my knowledge this was the only attempt ever made to research and record even a small portion of the Franz Michael Kunz ancestry and only came to light in a recent book published on the David Hager family by Margot Allred Hager, *Beginning at a Bounded White Oak*.[8] The work that Frank Llewellyn Hager left behind on the Hager family genealogy became the genesis for this book. Without the entry on Henry Michael Hager, descendent of the founder of Hagerstown, Maryland, and his wife, Elizabeth, in this book, it is quite certain that I would never have found the birthplace of our paternal ancestors, the Kunzes. Both Elizabeth and Henry Hager died in Dayton, Henry in 1925 and Elizabeth in 1926. They are buried in Memorial Park Dayton.

Mary, daughter of Franz Michael and Margaretha, was born in Dayton on September 9, 1858. She died in Delphos, Ohio, on June 23, 1916. Mary is the only one of the children who did not marry. She lived out her life quietly in Delphos and gained in the family quite a reputation for being eccentric. I recall my father saying that when someone in the family was acting a bit peculiar that they were acting "just like Aunt Mary." It is unfortunate that so little of her is remembered as she must have been a bit of a pioneer in her age to leave her parents' home and live out her life alone in a small town. She was Catholic and was buried in St. John's cemetery.

Philabena was born to the Kunzes in Dayton on July 12, 1862, just two years after Ferdinand our grandfather was born. She too moved to Delphos with her family and married Marion Thurston. The Thurstons had no children. Like her sister, she was Catholic and was buried in St. John's cemetery.

Barbara, the baby who made the trip on a sailing boat to America with her parents, died shortly after her parents made the move to Delphos on July 5, 1865. She was twelve years old. She is buried in the oldest section of the St. John's cemetery. The cause of her death is not known.

The last child to born to the Kunzes was Frank, born April 5, 1867, at their farm on McKibben Road. The Kunz siblings lived at home until they married – or, like Mary, until they finally sought their own independence. The boys of the family would have been required to learn their father's occupation. Frank was known in the community as a farmer and carpenter. He married Catherine "Kate" M. Shumaker October 25, 1893. The Frank Kunzes had three children. Frank Kunz died November 7, 1949 and is buried in the cemetery at St. John's in Delphos.

It can be assumed that our grandfather Ferdinand, who was only a small child when his parents made a decision to become farmers and move to the Delphos area, would have been thoroughly steeped in his father's dual occupations of farming and carpentry. The farm he grew up on is spacious and well-planned and provided the opportunity to practice both skills. Like his brother George, Ferdinand had a vision for his life than his siblings that differed from his siblings' aspirations.

Portrait of Ferdinand Kunz as a young man taken in Delphos, Ohio.

He would not choose to be a farmer who did some carpentry, but working with wood would be his life. He would become a designer, a builder, and a master craftsman, leaving behind examples of his work for the enjoyment of generations to come. Seven years older than Frank and surrounded by sisters that were still living at home, Ferdinand probably became the focus of his father's attention and had the opportunity to follow about in his father's footsteps as the house and barn and outbuildings were designed and constructed. Unfortunately, no written records exist of his youth, but somehow he became fascinated with the violin and became known a quite a "fiddler," playing at social events throughout his lifetime. Perhaps it was at one of these weddings or barn dances that our paternal grandparents met. Sadly, no one remains who could answer that question.

Whatever the circumstances of their meeting and courtship, Ferdinand Kunz and Deflora Clawson were married September 6, 1890 by Justice of the Peace D. E. Baxter at the Clawson residence on the Auglaize River.[9] Although the tintype picture of them on their wedding day is badly damaged, it is evident that Deflora inherited her mother's attractiveness.

This partially destroyed tintype portrait is a record of the wedding of Ferdinand and Deflora Kunz.

This portrait of Ferdinand and Deflora Kunz is believed to be an anniversary portrait. It is possible that it was taken a year or two after their wedding.

Ferdinand, tall and substantially built with dark curly hair, remained until his death in 1932 an imposing personage. It is believed that at first the couple resided with the Clawson family. Not far from the Clawson residence and a bit downstream, the couple managed to purchase a small farm in 1893. This piece of property remains in the Kunz family possession to this day.

A deed made to Frederick and Deflora designates the purchase of a triangular piece of land from the Peter Deihlman farm in Putnam County.[10] This property was bounded on two sides by the Pittsburg, Akron and Western Railway and Road U-20. A third side was bordered by a farm property now held by the Trentman family. Near the road and intersecting with a perpendicular road called the Dutch Road stood a large wooden structure which had been for many years a public elementary school called Brush College.

Class portrait of students of Brush College with a bit of the school's architecture displayed, possibly taken in the 1880s.

At the time the young couple purchased it, however, it was being used for various public functions and had been used in the recent past for Methodist church services. A new "Brush College," more spacious and constructed of brick, had been built to accommodate the elementary students of area, near a small village called Rushmore a few miles away.

Never a farmer at heart, Frederick "loaned out" his acreage to surrounding farmers for a portion of the profits. However, the Kunzes kept for themselves a large garden and planted many fruit trees and an abundance of berry bushes and flowers. They kept chickens and one horse called Old Ned, who pulled the buggy that took Ferdinand to his carpenter work and other work sites. Doubtless, Old Ned was used to transport the young couple to the homes of friends and relatives and other social occasions as well. Perhaps he even transported Ferdinand to his "fiddling" engagements, as he appears to have been quite in demand in his earlier years. He was also known for his great good sense of humor and generosity of spirit. Eventually Ferdinand became "Fred" to all who knew him or knew of him. The name Ferdinand had been left far behind.

Trained by his German father in carpentry, Ferdinand set about immediately to redesign and remodel the old schoolhouse into a comfortable family home for his wife Flo and the three children who would soon come, Eva, Edith, and Frederich (who was also known as Frederick and then Fred and Fritz as he grew older).

What had been a one-room schoolhouse became a cozy kitchen and dining room, a small separate living room and three bedrooms. A cistern and hand-dug well supplied the water for drinking and laundry. The cistern water was pumped into a small pantry off the kitchen. A kitchen range and an elaborate wood stove in the living room supplied the heating. All water was heated on the kitchen stove and kerosene lamps provided light. Across the front of the old school a porch was built and the traditional porch swing installed. Several outbuildings were eventually built for tools, the horse and buggy, and the chickens. (Until 1941 the space where the old school bell had hung was clearly visible in the ceiling of the largest bedroom, a square empty space covered over carefully with cheesecloth and papered over with layers of wallpaper.) Electricity came to the Kunz home by way of Rural Cooperatives in the middle 1930s, but indoor plumbing was not installed in the house until it was remodeled in 1941. (Please see Appendix B for a narrative of the transformation of Brush College into the Kunz family home.)

The Kunz home as it appears today on Road U-20, approximately five miles from Delphos, Ohio, and two miles from Fort Jennings, Ohio.

The Kunz home as it appeared after it had been converted from a school to a house.

The "real" building, however, took place outside these five acres as Ferdinand built houses and barns throughout the Delphos, Fort Jennings, and near Elida area. Many of these structures stand sturdy and strong today, now serving a second, third, or fourth generation of the original contracting family. The most illustrious of his structures was a round barn built on the Frank Moenter property at the intersections of the Lincoln Highway (US 30 N) and Lehmann Road (see Appendix C). This barn was constructed with a roof that was not attached to the sidewalls but instead literally levitated above the walls so as to withstand windstorms. This still fully functioning structure was torn down in 1976.

This round barn built by Ferdinand Kunz stood not far from Delphos, Ohio, until 1976 when it was destroyed.

Not being farmers, the Kunzes bartered for much of their food. They raised produce and fruit, chickens provided eggs and meat, but other meats and milk were traded for either carpentry work or butchering. When carpentry was not available, or the weather did not

89

permit construction, Ferdinand traveled about the countryside butchering animals for farmer families.

The contrast of lifestyles of the Frederick Lause II and the Ferdinand Kunz families would have been considered of some significance in the Catholic farming communities of the Delphos and Fort Jennings areas in the early twentieth century. The Lauses were considered independent farmers of substance and an integral part of the community brought to America by Reverend Bredeick. The Kunzes led the life of artisans dependent on others' needs for a livelihood. The Lauses were almost entirely self-sufficient in providing necessities for a large household. The Kunzes had to contract for, barter for, or do day work for their needs. For the Lause family, it was grinding hard work from sun up to sun set; all hands were needed to keep such a large family thriving on a relatively small farm. For the Kunzes, the lifestyle was not as grueling. There was time for talk, for fishing, for hunting, for reading and study. Nor did providing for the family *need* to be as difficult in the Kunz household as there were only three children spaced widely apart to be cared for.

There was no doubt about the religious traditions of the Lause family; their very reason for coming to America was to flee from religious persecution and bondage. For the Kunzes, the Catholic religion was a fairly new choice made after their arrival in America, perhaps even after their arrival in the Delphos area. Our paternal grandmother Deflora converted to the Catholic religion from Methodism in 1913 when she was forty-one, married, and the mother of three children. Both families attended St. John's Catholic Church in Delphos, but this was not the Kunzes' home parish. The Kunzes should have been members of the Fort Jennings Parish but they chose instead to travel further to attend services in Delphos, perhaps following the tradition started by the family when they first moved to the area. This decision, however, always set them somewhat apart from their Catholic neighbors and made them seem "different."

The children of both families in the main attended nearby country schools for their elementary schooling. The Lause children, however, attended the first two years of their schooling at the Catholic school in Delphos where they received their religious instruction in preparation for their First Communion. Thereafter, they attended country schools. Only the very youngest of the Lause children attended school in

Delphos on a regular basis after public transportation was provided. For the rest of the Kunz and Lause children it was a walk of two miles each way in all kinds of weather to attend either the country or Catholic school. There was no time or appropriate vehicle available to hard-working families to take their children to and from school. Our father's sister Edith Kunz recalled that when a new bridge was built over the Auglaize River, which flowed between their house and school, the men who were doing the construction work carried the children on their backs across the river. The only other alternative available to the children was to walk to the railroad tracks behind their property and walk the tracks across the railroad river bridge, then double back halfway to the school on the opposite side of the river. Just the thought of such alternatives would make present-day parents shudder, and perhaps the parents of the early twentieth century shuddered, too, but with no choice available, the risk had to be endured. Although limited in scope and length, formal education was held in highest importance by immigrant families who wanted the very best for their children. They saw education as the means of attaining goals they could never have dreamt of in the Old Country. Although some country school districts offered to pay tuition to area high schools for their students, few took advantage of this opportunity. By the end of the eighth grade, most of the students were destined to be trained in the occupations of their mothers and fathers. Indeed, most teachers of this early period did not have high school training but instead were required to pass a qualifying test which gave them the license to teach all the basic subjects in grades one through eight.

Notes

[1] The genealogical records held by St. John's Catholic Church in Delphos, Ohio, also proved useful for providing much of the information in this chapter.

[2] Records of the 118th Ohio Volunteer Infantry which was formed at Lima, Ohio, are held in the research department of the Delphos, Ohio Public Library.

[3] The ship *Lisbon's* arrival papers in New York are on file with the National Archives. However, to this date no record has been found of its departure from Le Havre, France. The *Lisbon* is believed to have been a sailing vessel.

[4] Statistical and genealogical materials relating to the Franz Michael Kunz and Margaretha Martz family are held at Jockrim, Germany, the equivalent of a "county seat" for the town of Rheinzabern, Germany.

[5] Immigration papers for Franz Michael Kunz are held in the State of Ohio Archives at Bowling Green State University, Bowling Green, Ohio. Margaretha was not required to seek citizenship.

[6] *Early Dayton* by Robert W. Steele and Mary Davies Steele provides a broad view of Dayton from its very beginnings to the late nineteenth century.

[7] George Kunz's article is on file at the University of Arkansas Library.

[8] For those who are pursuing the Hagerstown, Maryland, Hager line *Beginning at a Bounded White Oak* is a most valuable resource.

[9] The marriage certificate of Ferdinand Kunz and Deflora Clawson is on file at the Allen County Courthouse, Lima, Ohio.

[10] Copies of the Ferdinand Kunz deed materials are held at the Putnam County, Ohio Courthouse in Ottawa, Ohio.

Chapter Eight: Children of the River

The Auglaize River from the bridge which crosses it on Road U-20 looking toward Ft. Jennings.

As long as I can remember the Auglaize River, which lay within a half-mile of our family home, was always referred to as "the river." Walking to the river, fishing at the river, searching for Indian arrowheads down by the river, hunting along the river, swimming or skating or boating on the river – our activities and amusements were focused on the river. To cross the river, one had a choice of walking the rails to the railroad bridge or walking the road and crossing on the iron bridge which spanned the river. As children, my siblings and I knew nothing of the importance of the Auglaize River to our early ancestors; we just knew it was a destination for escape, where one could have fun and great adventures.

Our father Frederick Kunz never went for a Sunday afternoon walk along the river without bringing back some Indian artifact dropped on the riverbank generations ago by the various tribes that had used the Auglaize as their transportation lifeline while traveling from village to village or as a connecting waterway from Lake Erie to the Ohio River. On separate occasions he brought home a small china doll of the early nineteenth century and the leg of a Civil War era china doll, tiny mementos of early settler children who had also traveled the river. The Indian arrowheads, heavy grinding stones and large axe heads our father found were fascinating to us, and we learned to treat them with the same respect that he showed to them. The river and these various found bits of the past kindled in all of us a love of nature and a feeling of closeness to those who had shared the river before us.

The Auglaize River was an extension of the small five-acre farm we grew up on. The "real" farmers' children had hundreds of acres on which to play their games, whereas we had the river as a year-round companion for our fantasies and fun. I am sure we sensed that we were lucky to be such free spirits and have the river as an extension of our little property. The Auglaize River had played such a part in bringing together the elements of our heritage that we must have just felt born to it. Our parents strayed from it twice but ultimately came back to stay. A few years ago the railroad tracks that defined the one angle of the triangle boundary of our property were removed so that now one can only imagine the place where the tracks were and remember the blackberry bushes that once grew along the railroad embankment. The smell and taste of warm blackberries and the jam that our mother Viola made from them is harder to erase from one's memory than the metal and wood of the railroad tracks. The railroad bridge was destroyed also, and now all that is left of the magnificent stone and iron structure are great blocks of gray stone, resting on either side of the river in disarray. Gone is the indescribable thrill of squeezing through a small iron opening to stand on a stone support and huddle tightly against the bridge while a train passed by you only inches away. This was heady stuff and all part of being a child of the river as we viewed it, and rightly so. I stood absolutely terrified at the age of eleven when my nine-year-old brother Norman shouted to me from a distance of more than twenty feet above me where he was walking the narrow iron framework of the road bridge. He laughed at my fears and ignored my pleas to come down from there. It would have been at least a forty-foot fall to the river had he made a misstep.

But he made no misstep that day, and I am sure he climbed along that ironwork many times when I was not there to plead with him. He was, after all, a child of the river: he owned it, he knew it, and surely it would never do him harm.

This iron bridge was constructed over the Auglaize River in 1905-06.

Chapter Nine: Our Father, Frederich Kunz

It is reasonable to assume that our father, too, grew up a child of the river. His mother's ancestors had been tied to the Auglaize since 1828. His parents and grandparents lived along the river and were friends and neighbors. When Deflora and Ferdinand married in 1890, they lived with her parents on the river before obtaining a place of their own near the river three years later. They had lived in their converted schoolhouse twelve years before our father Frederich (also spelled Frederick) was born October 4, 1905. In the mean time, the Kunzes had given birth to two daughters, Eva on July 26, 1894, and Edith on May 25, 1900. In 1913 Deflora converted herself and her three children to the Catholic religion, and she and Ferdinand had their civil marriage validated by the Catholic Church. They were a close-knit family, and, as the youngest and the only son, Frederick was doted upon by his mother and father and especially by his two older sisters.

Portrait of Kunz children taken around 1910. Eva is on the left, Frederich in the middle and Edith on the right.

From family stories, it appears that our father led a protected and carefree life as a youngster. With no livestock to tend or vast fields to toil in, he could follow his own pursuits as a child. He attended a country school two miles away and across the river, as his older sisters had done. For the first few years of his schooling, he was taught a half-day in the German language and a half-day in English. The advent of World War I immediately stopped that practice just as it also stopped any speaking of German in the Kunz household. Great prejudice was shown toward German Americans during the war, and no one of German heritage wanted to attract undue attention by speaking German or reading German publications.

Frederich in his grade school classroom. He is in the middle row on the extreme left.

Frederick's interest in all things American Indian manifested itself in his grade school years. A story related in the book *One Room Schools of Putnam County, Ohio* tells of an incident when he and a neighbor boy, Frank Metzger, made a huge bow and arrow in school; the bow and arrow were so large that Frederick had to lie down to shoot, pulling the bow with his legs. The story speculates that the arrow was never found, so powerful was the shot. Making bows and arrows was a hobby that our father maintained throughout his life. I believe this interest was due, at least in part, to his fascination with the properties of various woods. For many years he scoured the river's edges for the wood of the Osage orange tree, which is an excellent choice for bow making.

Immediately after the end of his eighth grade school year he became an apprentice to his father in woodworking. This training with his master carpenter father put him in good stead for the other careers interests that would follow. Building houses, barns, outbuildings, and furniture generated in him a love of design, mathematics, and the use and handling of various materials. His life was not all work and study,

99

however; he became an avid fisherman and spent much of his free time walking the railroad tracks to the river to spend lazy afternoons fishing, alone or with neighboring farmer boys.

Frederich caught in his favorite pastime, fishing.

He was also an avid reader and "tinkerer" with all things mechanical. As a teenager he enrolled in a mechanical drawing correspondence course called "The T Square." This course laid the groundwork for his drafting and mechanical engineering abilities. When the automobile came into his life in his late teens, the whole world of auto mechanics opened to him, and he found he had a natural ability for doing repairs to the various automobile models that were available in the Delphos area. He acquired a series of automobiles in his late teens and early twenties which were his pride and joy. For a time he operated a mechanics garage in Delphos.

Frederich Kunz with two of the autos that he maintained.

Frederick had been a slight but generally healthy child. When he was twenty-one, he contracted measles, diphtheria, and scarlet fever back to back. Although he recovered from all these illnesses, this trauma led to physical weaknesses that would be manifested in his later life.

Somehow during his early twenties he came to the attention of B. J. Gramm, the owner of the manufacturing plant in Delphos and Lima that had produced the Liberty truck, which had been made famous by the U. S. Army in World War I.[1] Recognizing Frederick's abilities, Mr. Gramm took him on as a personal apprentice. At Gramm Motors Frederick further developed his knowledge of engineering and mathematics and learned for the first time to design entire vehicles. By 1929 Frederick was employed as a draftsman in the vehicle division of International Harvester in Fort Wayne, Indiana. Frederick never strayed far from the drawing board the rest of his life, even as his amazing mechanical and architectural abilities led him down many paths over the next forty-five years.

This is thought to be the last picture of Frederich with both of his parents. His father died in the winter of 1932 and this picture may have been taken the summer of 1931.

Notes

[1] *The Road to Liberty*, published by the Allen County Historical Society, gives an excellent history of the Gramm Motors Company and the invention of the "Liberty Truck."

Chapter Ten: Memories of Grandma Flo

A favorite spot of Flo Kunz's was her shady front porch. This picture was taken in the late 1930s.

At the very height of the Great Depression, our father Frederick Kunz lost his position as a designer at International Harvester in Fort Wayne, Indiana, as there was no demand for the vehicles that this plant produced in those lean years. It soon also became apparent that there were no jobs available for which our father was suited in the metropolitan area of Fort Wayne or in his hometown of Delphos. Our parents lost most everything. Buying things "on time" was at the height of its popularity during the Depression years, and this practice proved to be both a boon and a burden to young couples who were initially able to furnish their homes and then soon found themselves struggling to keep up with payments. Somehow Frederick and Viola managed to hold on to a few pieces of furniture, a large rug, a manual sewing machine and some small household goods. When the car was gone, Frederick walked the streets searching for work until the soles of his shoes were worn through. A sense of urgency fell upon them, as Viola was pregnant with Norman, their second child. Their choices were eliminated one by one, along with their possessions, over workless weeks, and with all reserves gone, the young couple had no choice but to return to their parents' homes in Ohio. At first they stayed with Viola's large family, but Frederick's father shortly became seriously ill and our parents felt they were needed more urgently to help at the Kunz household. And, indeed, they were.

Two weeks after their arrival at the Kunz home, our grandfather Ferdinand Kunz died, leaving his widow Flora and the house and little farm to be cared for. Flora's role in her new little family would be to care for the children – baby Norman, born two weeks after Ferdinand's death, and me, Winona – while our parents did day labor in the fields of the surrounding counties. Our grandmother, a woman of great pride, had forbidden our parents to seek "relief commodities" or governmental help. If they were to live under "her roof," they would respect her wishes. And they did so. By working long and backbreaking hard hours for very little pay, they somehow managed to secure food and life's other small necessities. Some necessities were bartered for carpentry work with farmers in the area. By this method, I suspect, a mysterious little silver pail of milk would be found on a nearby fence post in the mornings. The young couple's fortunes were improved a bit when Frederick managed to secure extension ladders and painting equipment and began painting houses and barns.

After more than four years of abject poverty, our family's lives were changed – by an upward turn that came on as suddenly as the downward turn had earlier – when Frederick was able to secure a position once again at International Harvester and move his little family back to the city.

Flora stayed on in the little house four more years until her daughter Edith closed her dry cleaning shop in Lima, secured employment in Delphos, and purchased a home on West Second Street. Flora joined Edith there, and they lived quite contentedly together until Flora's death of a stroke in 1943. Earlier in 1941 our paternal aunts, Edith and Eva, had signed over their share of the "home property" to their younger brother Frederick for a very nominal sum thereby assuring that the school-turned-house and its surrounding five acres would stay in the Kunz family name.

To gain something of a sense of what our father's life was like as he grew up, I have only my memories to reference for those years spent in his old environment. I was barely two when my family went to live in the little converted schoolhouse surrounded by farmland. For the next four and a half years, I was continually watched over by our paternal grandmother Flora who, incidentally, made it clear that she wished to be called not "grandmother" or "grandma" but by her nickname, Flo. Grandmother, she said, made her seem old, and having experienced our grandmother's playful and childlike nature, I quite agree with her decision. Most of my memories of those years are attached to some heightened or emotionally charged event, but some are quite as mundane as the smell of the cherry trees in bloom or the feel of a hot newly picked tomato in my hand. For the most part, people are shadowy figures who just provide backdrop for the real world, which consisted of three people, my grandmother, my brother, and me.

As children we were blissfully unaware of the hardships going on around us. Our grandmother became our world. She was by nature a kind, patient, and loving person. She made every day seem like fun and entered into our play as sincerely as a child. She would solemnly attend our play "weddings," "eat" the mud pies we served up in old jar lids, or spend hours reading and drawing with us. We soon found out, though, that she was no "softie" – if you violated a cardinal rule, like using a "bad" word, you would be punished. On one occasion I was dragged into the pantry where she furiously pumped water into my mouth as she washed it out with soap. Where I had learned "that word" at age five remains a mystery to me.

We had a favorite game we would play. Although we never gave it a name, it should have been rightly called, "Is the water just right yet?" After meals Flora would put all the dirty dishes in a pan of water on the kitchen range. If the range was not hot enough the water would be too cold to do the dishes, so into the stove would go more wood. We would be free to read our old tattered magazines, make paper dolls, or whatever else struck our fancy while the water heated. When we returned to the kitchen later, to nobody's surprise, the water in the pan was too hot, so we were "compelled" to go back to our more engaging pursuits while it cooled. This game could go on for hours it seems. It is a wonder to me that the dishes were ever done before the next meal, but I suppose that sometime in a lapse in the game Flora gave in and added some cold water to the water that was too hot to touch.

If we were short on food or a variety of foods, we did not know to ask about it. I do know, though, that as a small child I realized we had eggs for most main meals during the week and chicken on Sunday. I can remember clearly that if someone came down the road past our house on foot at mealtime our father would invite them in to share whatever we had. Our father always seemed pleased to talk with these travelers. Having worked for so long either in his own business or for a corporation, he must have greatly missed the conversations that he once had with customers and fellow workers.

We had no means of transportation but had to rely entirely on kind relatives or neighbors for the few family outings we experienced. My mother's sister Lucille, who lived in Lima, made my very favorite outing possible. Some Saturday evenings Lucille and her husband would pick us up in their auto and take us to the Lause home for a night of euchre-playing for the grown-ups and fun tearing through that many-roomed house for the grandchildren. There would be much laughter around the huge walnut dining room table as the aunts and uncles came together for their Saturday night ritual. Very late, perhaps after ten, Grandmother Lause would bring out big platters of homemade coffee cake and big pots of coffee for the adults and milk and cake for the little ones. There was so much warmth, laughter, and many good smells in those Saturday nights that they came to signify to me that all was not work in the Lause household. It was just that the family, born and bred of German peasant stock, worked hard and played hard – each in its appropriate time. A testament to this organizational and practical approach is the fact that our mother's parents brought eleven healthy and vigorous children into adulthood on a farm of less than forty acres, a feat that would be unheard of in today's farming culture.

Of my patchwork of memories that fill up those four and a half years spent on the Kunz farm near Fort Jennings, Ohio, some have remarkable clarity. I have a fleeting memory of sitting on my grandfather's knee in a big leather and wood chair in front of a window. I remember a fleeting moment, also, when the doctor who delivered my brother at home came out of my parents' bedroom and, obviously pleased, said to me, "You have a baby brother", and I, hugging a doll baby, replied, "I have a baby, too", and with some emphasis propped my doll up in a chair for him to see. One might think that such a competitive spirit with my yet unseen brother Norman might have led to sibling rivalry, but it did not. Those four years spent together with Norman, seldom seeing another child, created a bond between us that became the basis for a deep lifelong friendship.

Hazier and less focused are the memories of the days we spent playing together under the pear trees in the grassy back yard. The yard was surrounded by high bushy roses of every hue and rimmed on one side by black and red raspberry bushes. Could anything be more pleasant than a handful of warm red raspberries? Always in our bare feet, the bees that feasted on the fallen pears were our number one enemy, and Flora was kept busy making poultices of baking soda for our sting bites. Flora's knowledge of folk medicine was a godsend in a family where there was really no access to or money for doctors or dentists or hospitals. Fortunately, we all made it through our "exile" intact.

We numbered the hours of our days by the sound of a pendulum clock that sat high on a shelf in the kitchen. This clock, a handsome thing with a glass front and made of carved wood, had been a wedding present to Ferdinand and Flora. When our Aunt Edith passed on, this clock, with all its memories intact, came into my possession. I have only to wind it just a little and then I am immediately transported back to that kitchen with its green woodwork and linoleum floor and the big shiny teakettle heating on the kitchen range.

From a child's point of view, these were happy times. To be sure, there was a lack of playmates and close neighbors, but we were so busy with our "little plans" winter and summer we did not notice. And then there was always Grandma Flo to have fun with. Little things like cuts and bruises and bee stings we took in stride. Something big,

107

like walking the path to the outside toilet, was a scary thing and got all blown out of proportion. It did not help that on one occasion a harmless garter snake slithered across the path in front of me. I can still hear myself screaming at the very sight of it.

Fantastic things happened, too. On one occasion, our father Frederick, always the avid fisherman, brought home from a morning on the Auglaize River a bass fish that was so large that head to tip of tail it just fit the enamel top of our kitchen cupboard. Finding the creature in Loch Ness would have been no more amazing to us than this huge fish that seemed to swallow up our kitchen.

There were things, too, from a child's point of view that sent us into gales of laughter even though the adults around us might not have shared our view of the event. Such was the story of the horse Old Ned, kept as a something of a pet since he was no longer gainfully employed. One day Old Ned got loose, and to our mother's horror and our delight, started munching methodically on the freshly washed laundry hanging on the clothesline. Old Ned was severely reprimanded and put back in his barn. We children laughed ourselves silly. To this day, our mother cannot recall that tale without becoming a bit angry. And who could blame her? Clothes were few in those times, and the drudgery of washing on a board is not easily forgotten.

Although my brother Norman and I were only small children when we lived through "Our Depression," I believe we came out of it with some feeling for what our father's childhood had been like. Yes, there was hard work and life's necessities had to be met in one way or another, but there was also an easy flow to life. We had experienced Flora as "grandmother," but surely as "mother" she had treated Frederick similarly. There was no need here for the organization and structure that was an absolute necessity at the Lause household. The environment invited creativity, and, just as it had worked its magic on our father Frederick, it worked its magic on us.[1]

In the late 1920s, Frederich Kunz took this time-lapse picture of his mother
Deflora doing what she loved best, reading.

Notes

[1] All material in this chapter and the two that follow is drawn from the
author's personal experiences, family stories shared, and memories
long remembered and treasured.

Chapter Eleven: Our Mother, Viola Lause

Our mother Viola was born to Frederick Lause II (hereafter called Fred) and Lena Moreo on February 4, 1909, the fifth child and second girl in a family of nine boys and three girls.

All set for a Sunday afternoon outing, Frederick and Lena Lause proudly show off their children in their new buggy. The baby on Lena's lap is Viola.

In such a large family everyone had tasks they were required to carry out with very little exception. There was little time at the Lause home for idle pursuits but it was not a somber or cheerless place. Viola's parents were second generation Americans and still clung closely to the German values of order, discipline, and cleanliness. There was always good food, space to explore inside and out, and ready companionship with siblings near one's own age to be found in their home.

As I write this, our mother Viola has just passed her 94th birthday in good health and with a vigorous sharp mind and excellent memory. She has outlived all of her eleven siblings – two sisters (who died together in an auto accident in the early 1970s) and nine brothers.

Many times she has recounted to me some significant memories of her childhood until I can feel that I was there when she trudged off to school in the deep snow, heat or rain with her brothers teasing her all along the way. I have looked often in her memories for the light-heartedness of childhood, and most often all I see is responsibility and work and too little time for play, rest and opportunity for self-discovery. But then my thoughts are balanced by realizing that there was always laughter, the care and guidance of stern but loving parents, and the sense that "you were all in it together" from working the farm together. Farm survival has never been easy. Viola often found solace in her close friendship with her brother Frank.

As witnesses at a wedding in the late 1920s, Viola and her brother Frank chose to have their portrait taken to celebrate the occasion.

Born just sixteen months apart, they depended on each other and shared many of life's disappointments and joys as children and later as young adults.

Rising early as a young child, it was Viola's task to walk the cows to pasture two miles away; she then walked home, changed her clothes, and walked the two miles to school. In the evening after school the process would have to be repeated. I have traveled those routes with her, and I wonder if this was her opportunity to be alone, to enjoy nature, and her own thoughts, as she contemplated the school day ahead. She loved school and remembers her favorite teachers' names with great fondness. She remembers with some sadness that whenever a new baby was born to her mother, she would be taken out of school to help at home until her mother could manage the big brood again. Like Frederick Kunz, at the end of the eighth grade she was removed from school and brought home to help her mother with all the household tasks and childrearing. When Ohio passed a law that all children had to stay in school until they were sixteen, she and her siblings returned to the country school where they repeated the eighth grade until they turned sixteen. None but the youngest of the twelve children would have the opportunity for education beyond the eighth grade level.

Although not the eldest girl in the family, Viola was the most like her mother, and worked alongside her in all aspects of the cooking, cleaning, laundry, sewing, gardening, and dozens of other tasks that had to be performed to maintain this growing active family. She remembers that every morning year-round twelve or more loaves of bread would have to be baked from the dough set out the night before. Just slicing this bread for breakfast and school lunches was a difficult and time-consuming task.

Our grandmother Lena was of medium height and ample in stature. With all her dawn to dusk hard work, she retained her strong and solid German peasant appearance. Our grandfather Fred was a tall, well-proportioned man with a shock of black hair and drooping full mustache. Fred was born with one leg considerably shorter than the other, and he walked with a cane his entire life. This impediment, however, never stood in the way of his many years of working the farm behind a team of horses. He was a stern taskmaster, expecting as much from his children, especially the boys, as he willingly gave.

When Viola was just five years old, she contracted rheumatic fever and was bedridden for more than a year. Surely her illness must have added to her already over-burdened mother's work and worries. In 1915 the entire family, with the exception of two of the older children, George and Lucille, was stricken with smallpox. George and Lucille had been vaccinated at school and suffered such difficulty with the vaccinations that Fred had hesitated to have the rest of the family vaccinated. As a consequence, the two older children had to provide all the care for the entire family during their confinement. Miraculously, all survived with no further complications.

Holidays were always celebrated at the Lause home and there were presents and special foods for all at holiday time. Once a year a seamstress was hired to come and live with the family for a week. In that week she produced two sets of clothing for each child, one for everyday wear and the other for church and dress up. All undergarments were also handmade. Both the boys and girls eagerly looked forward to the seamstress's visit. Surely there were hand-me-downs in such a large group of children, but the prospect of having something new to wear that was one's own must have been exciting.

Another joyful visit was that of the female schoolteachers from the country school. The schoolteachers stayed a few nights each term in the homes of their students, especially if they lived at some distance and the weather was severe. The teacher always shared a bed with one of the girls and there was great excitement and vying over who would get to sleep with teacher. When it was my mother's turn, she said she was so excited that she could not sleep most of the night.

There were funny and exciting times, too. One Saturday Fred and Lena went to Delphos to buy supplies and left the older children in charge of the little ones. This was a time when Gypsies still roamed the back roads of Ohio. Scary tales of Gypsies stealing children, however false, were well known by the Lause children and most children of the time. A group of Gypsies entered the Lause barnyard with the Lause children watching terrified from the dining room windows. George, the eldest, now acting as the "man of the house," thinking quickly hid the smaller children in the huge pullout flour bin in the kitchen then boldly went out to see what the Gypsies wanted. The Gypsies politely asked to water their horses. Vastly relieved, George agreed and when the horses were watered he returned to the house. But what a sight, and what a mess, when the toddlers came tumbling out of the flour bin. Still, George was a hero from that day forward – the day he "saved" his siblings from being carried off and never seen again.

When motorcars became available, Fred purchased a Model T. However, he never bought a tractor, preferring to work with his horses until he finally retired from farming after World War II. Viola learned to operate the Ford by driving it in a circle in the barnyard. She did not learn to shift into reverse until many years later, and I am sure she never got to take the auto out of the barnyard onto the road.

By all accounts, Viola was a shy and quiet girl, always dutiful and hardworking. Her older sister Lucille, caring little for the domestic life, left home to "work out" as soon as she finished her schooling. Age sixteen was considered in the Lause household as something of a passage into adulthood, and to mark the occasion the girls were given the choice of an expensive piece of jewelry and allowed to seek work outside the home. Lucille chose a beautiful ruby ring with a diamond set in the center. Viola chose a white gold filigree wristwatch.

Viola and friends at the Lause home in the late twenties. Viola is in the middle, her sister Coletta in front of her and friends to either side.

Dutiful hardworking German girls were much in demand as maids in wealthy households in the nearby cities. Viola jumped at the opportunity to "work out" when she reached sixteen and took a position as a maid in the Burkemeir household in Delphos. She delighted in her first working experience away from home. Her delight was short-lived, however, as a new baby was on the way and she was needed at home. As had so often happened when Viola was a schoolgirl, when her mother became ill or overburdened, it fell to Viola to aid her mother in childrearing and the multitude of household duties until her mother could manage again on her own. After her mother's confinement and recovery, Viola returned to "working out" but never again to the family she was so fond of: that opportunity had passed. Instead, she obtained a position as maid to a wealthy family named Mackenzie in Lima, Ohio.

She tells with delight her thrill at having her own pretty bedroom and being treated with respect by her employers and her fellow servants. The Mackenzies employed a black chauffeur, and for the first time in her life Viola became friends with someone from a culture different from that of her German American background. She was very happy in her position and hoped for a long stay in the Mackenzie household. Her younger sister Coletta also took a position with one of the founding families of Lima, so the sisters had contact with each other on a regular basis as they took walks through the affluent neighborhoods. Viola tells an amusing story of Coletta, always the actress. Viola and Coletta accidentally met on a street corner while Coletta was walking her employer's dog. Coletta pleaded with Viola not to reveal her identity as she was pretending to all she met that she was the daughter of the wealthy family she worked for. Stung at being "disowned" by her sister, Viola nonetheless kept Coletta's secret and moved on pretending that they did not know each other.

Viola stayed in her position at the Mackenzies until her fiancé, Frederick Kunz, obtained a position at International Harvester in Fort Wayne, Indiana. In the late twenties the distance of 73 miles between Fort Wayne and Lima seemed daunting to the young couple. To remedy the situation, Viola left the Mackenzie household and, with their recommendations in hand, secured a position with a family in Fort Wayne. She took up residence in the home of a young married couple who became friends to Viola and Frederick and in 1929 were the witnesses to their marriage.

Chapter Twelve: Memories of Grandma Lena

I learned something of what my mother's childhood must have been like when, at the age of eight or nine, I was sent by my parents to spend part of the summer with my Grandmother and Grandfather Lause on their farm near Delphos, Ohio. Although I had spent a good deal of my earliest years on the little Kunz "farm," the thought of spending time on a "real" farm was most exciting, and I eagerly left

The Frederick Lause II homestead on State Road 66 two miles from Delphos, Ohio. Picture taken in the 1940s.

Fort Wayne behind to learn what it was like to be a real "farm girl." I very shortly learned that I was not just "the little visitor from the city" but was expected to pitch in and learn just as my mother had. Grandmother Lena was kind and fair and fun to spend time with, but she tolerated no shirkers, no matter what age, in her environment.

Donald, the youngest of my mother's brothers was still a teenager living at home, and he tended the animals and worked the fields with my grandfather. The older sons had left the farm for other occupations or farms of their own after the worst of the Depression years were over. During the week my grandmother and I did not see much of "the men" except at mealtimes and for a short time after dinner. Donald was a cheerful boy, full of fun, who loved to tease. He never passed up an opportunity to tell me some wild tale about the cows as we walked them to the fields. His storytelling skills were considerably sharpened by the gullibility of the listener. (I imagine now that my mother and her brother Frank might also have shared such outrageous stories and laughter as they went about their daily chores.) On one occasion while watering the workhorses at the watering trough, Donald convinced me that the long skinny hair-like worms in the water were really long hairs from the horse's tails and manes that had fallen into the water and became living creatures. For many years after – in truth, to this day – that story still haunted me.

My day started with a call from my Grandmother at 5:30 a.m. to get up. The sun was rising, the roosters crowing, but I felt as if my head had just touched the pillow. There was no time for anything except to hurriedly jump into my clothes and make a mad dash for the outside toilet (the indoor plumbing not yet having been completely installed) and report to the kitchen. My grandfather and uncle were already in the barn milking the cows, putting down oats and hay for the horses, feeding the pigs, and doing all the many chores that were necessary before they harnessed the horses for the day's work in the fields. Our first task before breakfast was to go to the garden with pails and pans in hand to gather vegetables that needed picking, pulling, or digging. Once satisfied that we had gathered all the vegetables we could use, can, or pickle that day, we picked the berries and cherries that had ripened since the previous day. Having accomplished all this before the sun became unbearably hot in the humid northern Ohio summer, we set off with our booty to get breakfast ready for the four of us and any family member or neighbor who might drop by.

The kitchen immediately took on a life of its own: the fire in the cook stove was tended, home-cured bacon and fresh eggs brought from the downstairs larder, a big pot of coffee made, homemade bread sliced, and a saucepan of oatmeal set cooking. I was given the privilege of setting the table and getting out the butter, jams and sugar from a little cupboard built into the kitchen wall. My delight was taking carefully from the cupboard the butter dish, sugar bowl, and spoon holder, each of cobalt blue glass trimmed with gold. Caught in such plain and solid surroundings, their beauty seemed even more pronounced to me. Today those items, given to me as a young wife and mother, grace my kitchen and never fail to bring back memories of the big hearty breakfasts which to most city dwellers would have been in sufficient quantity to serve for a day's meals but here was only a prelude to lunch, a real meal ready at 11:30 a.m.

I can only speculate how things were managed in the Lause household when there were many more times children around the table. The key to surviving, it seems, was our grandmother's sense of organization and management; a sense that did not waver even though the number of those to be fed had decreased. This must have been a difficult adjustment for Lena who had depended also on those same willing hands to help keep her "machine" well oiled. As humble as my assistance was that summer, I did feel a genuine sense of appreciation that I had at least tried for a little while to "stand in" for her daughter Viola.

The times between meals were taken up with preparing and canning fruits and vegetables, baking, sewing and mending, and always cleaning up. My grandfather always listened to the radio news after lunch. Well, "listened" is probably not the appropriate verb. He was a dyed-in-the-wool Roosevelt Democrat and took issue with anything that veered from the "Party Line." Sitting in his favorite chair next to the tabletop radio with his cane in hand, he would talk back to the radio commentator, almost constantly it seemed, pounding the cane hard on the floor if he was especially upset. I suppose as a child I should have been frightened at such behavior from this big and powerfully strong man, but I was not. Instead I felt proud that he knew and cared so much about what affected his life as a farmer. I learned a lot about how excited people can get about politics and opinion that summer.

After dinner and the dishes I would try to seize the opportunity for some fun in my structured day. I loved playing cards, especially euchre which is very popular in the German American communities of northwest Ohio. After much pleading on my part and teasing on my grandmother's part, we would settle down to play. At 7:30 p.m. the clock on the dining room sideboard would chime and that dreaded sentence, "Off to bed with you now," would come on cue from my grandmother. No amount of pleading for just one more game would do. After all, like any good manager who has observed over the years what does and does not work, she knew that little girls who must arise at 5:30 a.m. must be in bed at 7:30 p.m. It was this realization, as I lay wide awake far beyond 7:30 p.m. in the still light of day, that helped me decide at a very tender age that farm life probably would not top the list of my life's priorities. I also understood why my mother and her sisters set their eyes on "working out" at sixteen. Life without time for euchre ran the risk of being no life at all, I concluded.

One of the most memorable moments in my grandmother's kitchen was the day I got to make a hickory nut cake "from scratch." The occasion was my grandfather's birthday, and my parents and younger siblings were driving from Fort Wayne to visit. Hours were spent cracking the nuts with a hammer against a stone, and then picking out the nutmeat with a tine of a fork. Once this ritual was finished, I was ready for the real challenge of making a yellow cake from batter, oven, to homemade icing. I am fully convinced now that my Grandma Lause with her organizational skills could have been the manager of a large corporation, and I also credit her with being a great teacher. And, like a good administrator or teacher, she knew how to delegate to those she trusted. I am proud to say the cake in all its aspects was perfect, and I fairly burst with pride serving it to my family. The annoyance of arising at 5:30 a.m. and not getting to play cards often enough paled when my grandmother complimented my accomplishments to my parents.

Perhaps, I was never going to be a farm girl or a domestic, but that summer I learned some very important things about the role of strong women in building a new society.

To celebrate their fiftieth wedding anniversary, Frederick and Lena had their portrait taken in Delphos, Ohio.

Chapter Thirteen: Coming Together

Frederich Kunz at age two.

The story of our parents' meeting has long fascinated me, and I feel most fortunate to have my mother to talk to and wonder together about it. Like the beginning of all love stories, it has a good bit of serendipity and magic, and I am charmed by it each time I hear it.

Viola Lause at age two.

Our father's sisters Eva and Edith were a good bit older than he; Eva by twelve years and Edith by six. As a consequence, when Frederick was in his teens Eva had already married and Edith had left home to follow a career that took her to Lima during the weekdays. Eva had married a young man named Ben Osting, who had been her schoolmate in the one-room school across the river. Eva and Ben bought the farm directly across two large fields from the Kunz property. Ben was an active farmer and before his own five sons were of an age to help in the fields he employed hired hands. How it came that he hired our mother's eldest brother George is unknown to my mother. Since the Kunz and the Osting farms were so close to each other, it was only natural that George came to know all three of the Kunz children in one capacity or another. Edith Kunz and George Lause became quite close friends.

Frederich Kunz's First Communion portrait.

On a Sunday afternoon George and Edith decided to take a buggy ride. Although this was the era of the early automobile, most families who kept horses retained their buggy and embraced it as a convenient and safe means for the occasional "old-fashioned" buggy ride for young people. On this particular day George and Edith decided to visit the Lause family near Delphos and, in a spirit of generosity, decided to take young Frederick along. Frederick would have been sixteen and Viola twelve on this sunny Sunday afternoon in 1921.

Viola Lause's First Communion portrait.

Viola was an incredibly shy and quiet child and found it difficult to relate to others outside the family. But on this particular day something magical was happening in her life. When the young people drove into the Lause barnyard, the three of them in a three-seater buggy, the Lause children were at hand to greet them. Intent on taking an even further jaunt, Frederick asked, "Would anyone like to ride along?" Realizing full well that she would have to sit on Frederick's lap to do so, the suddenly transformed Viola said quite simply, "I would." More than eighty years after her sudden burst of courage, Viola still marvels at her audacity. In just two words, the worlds of Viola Lause and Frederick Kunz were brought together. With this simple gesture, the elements of all our ancestors' backgrounds – so many lands, so many languages, so many religions, so many cultures – were destined to come together. Although courtship and marriage were years in the offing, on that day each unknowingly chose a life's mate.

Frederich Kunz dressed in cowboy garb in the late 1920s.

Viola Lause with borrowed hat and bandana "playing cowboy" in the late 1920s.

This Willys Overland auto was Frederick Kunz's pride and joy.

Viola Lause "cutting up" a bit next to one of Frederich's treasured autos.

Always dapper, Frederich shows off his new straw hat as Viola's parents look on with laughter from their front porch.

Viola Lause in a bridesmaid portrait taken as she witnessed a friend's wedding in the late 1920s.

So now the die was cast: generations from England, Germany, Holland – Protestant and Catholic, farmer and townsmen, affluent and barely middle class – had come together in this one moment in those almost whispered utterance, "I would." The year of the momentous buggy ride was 1921. It would be eight years before Frederick and Viola married. The difficulties of immigrant settlement, interactions with Native peoples, laying claim to and taming the lands opened by treaty or military conflict, the War of 1812, and the Civil War were now only distant memories relegated to the past and the reminiscences of a few aged relatives. No one in our parents' immediate families had fought in World War I as all the fathers were too old for military duty and the sons too young during the crucial war years, and as a consequence they had been spared the horrors of that war. From family stories and old photographs, one could surmise that the Kunz/Lause families, like most American families of that era, were focused on the future. The Great Depression was almost a decade away. The culture was changing as most area German newspapers had gone out of existence because of the prejudice exhibited against the German Americans during the War. The German language was no longer taught in the little country schools our parents attended, ending the era of German bilingualism and, in effect, cutting the ties to the Old Country. Frederick's and Viola's formative years were decidedly English speaking, "American," and focused on the dream of upward mobility. Turbulent times would lie ahead for them and for all young people of their generation. But in the early 1920s all eyes were set forward, and Frederick and Viola, like most young people of that era, seldom looked back.

The young married couple, Frederich and Viola Kunz, on the front porch of their house in Ohio, early 1930's.

Suggested Readings

—————————. *History of Allen County, Ohio*. Chicago: Warner, Beers and Co., 1885.

—————————. *History of Montgomery County, Ohio*. Reprint. Evansville, IN: Unigraphic, Inc., 1971.

Banta, R. E. *The Ohio*. New York: Rinehart and Company, 1949.

Bicentennial Committee. *Delphos Vicenqui-Bicentennial Historical Book*. Delphos: Ohio, 1976.

Carnes, John R., Ed. *The 1976 History of Allen County, Ohio*. Evansville, IN: Unigraphic, Inc., 1976.

Clawson, Charles W. *Thomas Clawson and Allied Families*. Fort Wayne, IN: n.p., 2002.

Covault, Richard. *Descendents of Covalt, Covault, Cavolt, Their History and Genealogy in America 1714-1900*. Sun City, AZ: n.p., 1990.

Delphos Canal Commission. *Reflections 1812-1960, A Pictorial History of Delphos, Landeck, Ottoville, and Fort Jennings, Ohio*. Virginia Beach, VA: Donning Company Publishers, 2000.

Eckert, Allan W. *A Sorrow in Our Heart*. New York: Konecky and Konecky, 1992.

Eckert, Allan W. *That Dark and Bloody River*. New York: Bantam Books, 1996.

Fort Jennings Bicentennial Committee, *Historical Fort Jennings 1812-1976*. N.p: n.p, 1976.

Galloway, William Albert. *Old Chillicothe, Shawnee and Pioneer History*. Zenia, OH: The Buckeye Press, 1934.

Gilbert, Bill. *God Gave Us This Country: Tekamthi and the First American Civil War*. New York: Athenum, 1989.

Hackman, Frank. *It Happened Here: Portraits of the Great Black Swamp*. Lima, OH: Franklee Publishing, 1958.

Hager, Margot Allred. *Beginning at a Bounded White Oak: A History of David Hager and his Descendents*. Bountiful, UT: Family History Publishers, 1997.

Hartshorn, Derick S., III. *The Hartshorn Families in America*. Baltimore: Gateway Press, 1997.

Harvey, Henry. *History of the Shawnee Indians, From the Years 1681 to 1854 Inclusive*. Cincinnati: Ephraim Morgan and Sons, 1855.

Heckewelder, John. *History, Manners, and Customs of the Indian Nations*. Reprint. New York: Arno Press, 1971.

Hill, Leonard V. *John Johnson and the Indians*. Columbus, OH: Stoneman Press, 1957.

Kamp, Gayle O. *The Kamp Papers, Vol. II*. Amarillo, TX: Staked Plains Publishers, 1986.

Miller, Charles C., Ed. *History of Allen County, Ohio and Representative Citizens*. Chicago: Richmond and Arnold Publishers, 1906.

Putnam County Historical Society. *History of Putnam County Ohio*. 1880. Evansville, IN: Unigraphic Press, Inc., 1976.

Putnam County Historical Society. *Putnam County Pioneer Reminiscences, Number One and Two*. 1878 and 1887. Kalida, OH: n.p., 1981.

Rusler, William. *The Standard History of Allen County*, Chicago; New York: The American Historical Society, 1921.

Russell, Donald and Janice Russell. *Russell Family History.* ms. Private Collection, 1992.

Scamyhorn, Richard and John Steinle. *Stockades in the Wilderness*. Dayton, OH: Landfall Press, 1986.

Scheeley, Mary L., Ed. *Putnam County, Ohio One Room Schools*. Mt. Vernon, IN: Windmill Publications, 1990.

Selfridge, Anna. "The Road to Liberty." *The Allen County Reporter* Vol. LVIII, No. 2, 2002.

Steele, Robert W. and Mary Davies Steele. *Early Dayton*. 1896. Bowie, MD: Heritage Books, Inc., 1999.

Sugden, John. *Tecumseh, A Life*. New York: Henry Holt and Company, 1997.

Susanna Russell Chapter of the Daughters of the American Revolution. *Blackhoof, Warrior in Winter*. Wapakoneta, OH: n.p., 1974.

Thom, James Alexander. *Panther in the Sky*. New York: Ballantine Books, 1989.

The Centennial Committee. *The Centenary of St. John the Evangelist Church*. Delphos: OH: n.p., 1981.

The Delphos Canal Commission. *Samuel Forrer, Absentee Landlord*. N.p.: n.p., n.d.

Vasko, Rev. Christopher. *Reverend John Otto Bredeich*. Delphos, OH: n.p., 1989.

Wallace, Paul A.W. *Indians in Pennsylvania*. Harrisburg, PA: Pennsylvania Historical and Museum Commission, 1981.

Williamson, C. W. *History of Western Ohio and Auglaize County*. Wapakoneta, OH: C. W. M. Linn and Sons Press, 1905.

Winter, Nevin O. *A History of Northwest Ohio, Vol. I*. Chicago, New York: Lewis Publishing Company, 1917.

Zeisberger, David. *History of the Northern American Indians*. 1910. New York: Arthur W. McGraw, 1991.

Appendix A: Josiah Clawson's Battle Experience

Josiah Clawson
118th Regiment Ohio Volunteer Infantry

List of Battles:

Massey Creek, TN	12/29/1863
Rocky Face Ridge, GA	5/ - 5/9/1864
Resaca, GA	5/13 – 16/1864
Dallas, GA	5/25 – 6/4/1864
Kennesaw Mountain, GA	6/9 – 30/1864
Kennesaw General Assault	6/27/1864
Siege of Atlanta, GA	7/28 – 9/2/64
Waynesboro, GA	11/27 – 29/1864
Franklin, TN	11/30/1864
Nashville, TN	12/15 – 16/1864
Fort Anderson, NC	2/18/1865
Town Creek, NC	2/20/1865
Mosely Hall, NC	4/9/1865

Appendix B: A Hundred Years Of Building Tradition: 1893-1993

Winona Garmhausen, Ph.D.

November 25, 1893: *Ferdinand and Deflora (Clawson) Kunz, lately of the Defiance Trail, today purchased a five-acre triangular portion of Peter Deihlman's farm in Putnam County. This property is bounded on one side by the Pittsburg, Akron and Western Railway and on another by Road U 20. The old Brush College public school rests on the Kunz's newly acquired property near the intersections of Road U 20 and Road 22. This building has recently been used for community functions. Ferdinand and Deflora were married in September of 1890 at the Clawson home on the Defiance Trail. They are the children of Franz Michael and Margaretha (Martz) Kunz, farmers of Kiggins Road near Delphos, and Josiah and Malinda (Hartshorn) Clawson, Jr., merchants and farmers.*

Although the above "news item" is not actual but has been gleaned through a study of our families' history, it is fact, and it does set the stage for a century of building by the Kunz family, emanating from the base of five acres and the old school tucked away between large and productive farms.

Ferdinand (Fred), trained by his German father in carpentry and farming, set about immediately to redesign and remodel the old school into a comfortable family home for his wife and the three children who were to come, Eva, Edith and Frederich.

What had been a one-room schoolhouse became a cozy kitchen-dining room, a small separate living room and three bedrooms. A cistern and hand-dug well supplied the water for drinking and laundry. The cistern water was pumped into a small pantry off the kitchen. A kitchen range and an elaborate wood stove in the living room supplied the heating. Across the front of the old school a porch was built and the traditional porch swing installed. Several outbuildings eventually were built for tools, the horse and buggy, and the chickens. (Until 1941 the space where the school bell had hung was clearly visible in the ceiling of the largest bedroom, a square empty space covered over carefully with cheese cloth and papered over with layers of wallpaper.)

The "real" building, however, took place outside these five acres as Ferdinand built houses and barns throughout the Delphos, Fort Jennings and Elida area. Many of these structures stand sturdy and strong today, now serving a second, third, or fourth generation of the original contracting family. The most illustrious of his structures was a round barn built on the Frank Moenter property at the intersections of the Lincoln Highway (US 30 N) and Lehmann Road. (See Appendix C) This barn was constructed with a roof that was not attached to the sidewalls but instead literally levitated above the walls so as to withstand windstorms. This still fully functional structure was later torn down. When building was not possible, Ferdinand traveled about butchering for area farmers. He was a tall, substantially built man, known throughout the area for his "fiddle playing", humor, and generosity of spirit. He died quite suddenly in 1932 in the little house he had fashioned bit by bit from the old school. His widow, known to all as "Flo," lived on in the little house until 1940.

In 1929 Ferdinand's son, Frederich (Fritz) married Viola Lause, daughter of Frederick and Lena (Moreo) Lause. Frederich and Viola made their home in Fort Wayne, Indiana, where Frederich was employed by International Harvester in the vehicle design department. A daughter, Winona, was born during these years. For a time during the height of the Depression they returned to live with Deflora in her home. A son, Norman, was born to Frederich and Viola in the family home, shortly after they returned to Putnam County. Frederich provided for his mother and wife and two children, as his father had done before him, by building and re-building for others in the area. In 1936 Frederich returned to International Harvester where he further developed his love of designing specialized vehicles. Looming World War II was already creating demands for vehicles suited to various military purposes.

In 1940 Frederich made the decision to move his family, now enlarged by two additional children, Sylvia and Ronald, away from the city and back to his family home near Fort Jennings. His mother and sisters, happy to see the Kunz building tradition continued, relinquished their shares in the property to him. Deflora and daughter

Edith purchased a home on East Second Street in Delphos where they lived together until Flora's death in 1943. In less than a year Frederich resigned from International Harvester to design and develop military and transport vehicles for Gramm Trailers in Delphos. World War II had just begun.

Frederich, like his father before him, had been trained from an early age in the art of carpentry. Shortly after finishing the eighth grade at the little school across the Auglaize River, Frederich began to build along side his father. High school was not an option for him so he worked with his father by day and studied mathematics and a home study course in the "T-Square" by night. He had a natural bent for mechanical things and the new and intriguing automobiles that Detroit was producing. This interest led him to operating a mechanic's garage in Delphos, an apprenticeship in drafting at the T. J. Gramm Company, and eventually to the design department at International Harvester. But the love for carpentry was always there and came out in our family home before all else.

In 1940 the old school house began to under-go the second of its transformations. The "Brush College" house found itself picked up, turned around and set over a basement far from its original position near the road. Then the remodeling began in earnest. Turned around and raised up, the old school soon became a model of modernity. A breakfast nook was added, a functional fireplace built of brick inside and out, a second floor created from the attic, the porch enclosed and a stairwell, frosted glass bordered, to lead to the new space upstairs. The focus of the house, however, became the oversized picture window. An innovation at the time, the picture window and glassed-in staircase attracted many people who came to stare and inquire about its construction and significance. The old outbuildings disappeared, a modern garage shot up, and later a shelter house of log construction was built for family picnics. Trees which had once densely backed the old school were replaced by 1000 spruce and fir seedlings and in time provided a small forest beyond the house and lawns.

As children, my brothers, sister, and I grew up in a swirl of plaster dust and sheets being hung to designate a new and mysterious room. It seemed to us that our father was destined to forever move, hammer, plaster, wire, plumb, shingle, and re-arrange our surroundings. After all, in our house "remodeling" was a tradition and we were certain that he wouldn't quit until he had tried all his ideas out first in his "home laboratory." This tradition could be counted on to bring wonder and amazement to our extended family and neighbors. It was not amazing to us that all these changes were accomplished in his "spare time." We just assumed that everyone's father came home from work, changed his clothes, at a bite and settled down to his "real" work. We knew that our father went off each day to Delphos and Lima to design and invent vehicles for Gramm Trailers and later to design buildings and nursing homes for the Wolfe Brothers at Lima Lumber, but those were the abstract stories told round the dinner table. His real work, the work that we absorbed by imitation and day-to day exposure was the world of tools, wood, mortar, and the heady acrid smell of plaster drying. Our younger brothers Larry and Steven, born to a home already transformed to its "newest" self, didn't miss out on the fun either. Their arrivals signaled another bedroom to be squeezed out of the attic followed by a complete "remodel" of the kitchen and bath and the rectangular breakfast nook into a circular formation.

When it seemed that the house just couldn't take any further change, Frederich turned to constructing furniture and a big wooden boat with an inboard Cadillac engine which we raced up and down the Auglaize River at Five Span. Truly the sawdust never settled on our five acres. Frederich died in his sleep on a warm night in July of 1974 in the house had had conjured in his imagination. A tall, quiet, introspective and well-read man, he was many things to many people. Some knew him for his love of horticulture, some for his interest in lapidary and jewelry making, others for his mechanical inventions and designs, and still others knew him by the homes, commercial buildings, and nursing homes he created. We knew him as a man who built for himself and his family "in his spare time." His widow Viola continues to live on in the little house on five acres that her husband so carefully shaped for her.

I doubt that my five siblings or I ever said consciously, "When I grow up I want to remodel and build buildings." We had learned about that part of ourselves from the experiences of our environment. Only later after other career turns and twists did this love come back, and in varying levels and different ways. In time, Norman and Ronald of Delphos formed an informal "partnership" and built and remodeled together as their father had "in their spare time." Many families and businesses in the Delphos area can lay claim to their building efforts. Meanwhile Ronald continues to oversee the construction and maintenance of all Allen County Public buildings. Steven of Fort Jennings received a degree in architectural design. When Frederich retired from his architectural position, Steven was prepared to take the reins from his father. Steven continues to design and supervise the construction of commercial and public buildings in Northwest Ohio. Each of the other three children has manifested this love of working with one's hands in other ways: Larry in manufacturing, Sylvia in nursing, and Winona in the arts. All, however, are intimately involved in the physical aspects of their homes whether it is design, execution, or the appreciation of quality workmanship.

As Frederich and Viola's grandchildren come into their own, two have already emerged in the building field. Norman's son works in construction in Cincinnati and especially enjoys teaching less experienced workers woodworking skills. Jill, Winona's daughter, has designed five houses in Santa Fe, New Mexico, and has personally supervised the construction of three of the five. No doubt in time, others will follow. It has been said that every skilled craftsperson had five generations of craftspeople in his or her family ancestry. If this is the case, then we all owe tremendous thanks to Franz Michael Kunz, who was born and reared amongst the forests on the Rhine River in Germany, for the precious and lasting gift he passed on to us.

As to the old Brush College, whose spirit rests quietly inside the Kunz family home, it remains to be seen what additional transformation the next century will bring.

Author's Note: This article was originally published by the Putnam County Historical Society in their Newsletter No. 62 (pp. 1-5) in August of 1995 and is reprinted here with their kind permission.

Appendix C: No Corners Cut On Moenter Barn

Mark Wert
The Daily Herald
Friday, June 14, 1974
Page 7

They just didn't understand. They thought he was trying to be different, they thought he was a fool; they tried to talk him out of it. But that didn't stop him. Frank Moenter built his round barn anyway. Sixty years later, Mr. Moenter's son Elmer continues to use the barn which remains a curiosity today.

Mr. Moenter had either feeder or dairy cattle in the barn for many years. He says, "It was a wonderful barn for livestock." But then came years of declining profits. Now all the barn holds is some machinery, two cats and a dog. Mr. Moenter and his wife live on the Rt. 2 farm which Mr. Moenter's father acquired by trading with another farmer. When it came time to build a barn, Frank Moenter wanted the round barn for two reasons: he could build two tracks around the rafters to move loose hay stored in the barn's mows and the barn was a little more wind resistant.

The plans for the 60 feet in diameter (200 feet in circumference) barn were all ready to go when the first carpenter Frank Moenter could convince to take the job, John Wert of Van Wert, became ill and died. Mr. Moenter's father had to make another long search until he finally found another person willing to take on the ambitious project. Fred Kuntz (Frederich Kunz) was the man who finally built the barn. Mr. Moenter says "they planned and planned how they were gonna build it."

Oak and ash —— "good native wood" were used to build the barn. The barn's rafters were constructed on the ground and then raised up by poles and pulleys to the main roof's wheel, supported by a 60-foot gin pole. The barn's roof is 54 feet up from the basement floor; the basement is three feet underground.

The roof's studs are 30 inches apart where the roof begins and taper in to three inches apart above the main ring. There are no posts holding the lofty roof up. It just holds itself up, Mr. Moenter says. Looking at the barn from the outside the old style bank up to the front doors is a tip-off to the barn's age. There are two covered inclines to the basement on the east and west sides of the barn. Although it appears small on the outside, the round barn has quite a massive interior.

A round barn is quite functional besides being strikingly unique in appearance. Joseph Dunlap, curator of the Allen County Museum in Lima, says the idea of round or octagonal homes and barns became very popular in the 1880s. He says they were primarily built because they would use up to 25 percent less construction material than a building of conventional design while still yielding the same amount of space inside. Mr. Dunlap adds that there are two other round barns in Allen County.

On the basement level, there is a large area where Mr. Moenter had milking stalls for his dairy herd. A milk pump still hangs in the basement from his dairy days. Besides all the space, the basement maintained good temperatures for livestock, cool in the summer and warm in the winter. "Some fellers said they couldn't stand goin' out and milkin' in the cold," Mr. Moenter says, "but I like it. Gave me something to do in the winter."

It's a short walk up the curved ramp to the main floor. Mr. Moenter now stores some of his machinery here but at one time kept as much as 40 tons of loose hay in the barn's two mows in addition to a large mound of corn fodder on the two inch floor. By using the cars in the two tracks, "you can dump (hay) almost anywhere in the barn." Mr. Moenter just can't get most of today's wider equipment in the barn. "For what I need it for," he says, "it isn't any good." But he adds, "You just can't tear the barn down."

He doesn't know how much the barn cost to build but he does know "it's gonna cost a lot to keep." Mr. Moenter is now faced with the problem of having the roof reshingled. The barn's red lock shingles were put on 35 years ago over the barn's original wooden shingle roof. When some of the red shingles began to come off, Mr. Moenter tried to get the same type of shingles to replace those that had cracked off and blown away. He was told they were no longer made. "Why can't they keep on with the same kind of shingles?," he laments. Although the cost of a new roof will be high, he and his wife can hardly stand the replacement shingles, which he says "stand out like a sore thumb." While the wind may take off some shingles now and then, the barn itself has weathered some strong winds.

Mr. Moenter remembers the severe storm that destroyed the Landeck church in 1948. After having been downstairs milking, he came upstairs. "That cupola was standin' there shakin'," he says. He stood and watched the whole roof move in the wind and then quickly went back to the basement. No damage was done to the barn. Several years ago, Mr. Moenter had a cousin strengthen the cupola, which was becoming very loose, with several braces.

When Route 30 North was built, the Moenters thought for a while that the road would be much further east of their barnyard. The final plans brought the state's right-of-way within 12 feet of the barn's east side and took 125 acres of the Moenter's land. Tom Schroeder, district real estate engineer for the Ohio Department of Transportation, says that no more land will be purchased from the Moenters. The Moenters will lose the trees in front of their house soon, though. The embankment for the overpass over 30 N will go right past the Moenter's front window.

People traveling along on Route 30 will often stop to take a picture of the barn or even stop and ask if they can walk through it. Mr. Moenter tells the story about a retired couple from Kansas who stopped when the Moenters were painting the barn. He recalls they said, "We got to look at your barn. We got a round barn and our cupola blew off."

The Moenter's showed the around the barn and when they came to the ramp to the upstairs, the wife said, "Lookit here, Pop, they don't have to climb a ladder like we do."

The barn was pictured in a section of oddities in Ohio on a map produced by the State Highway Department several years ago. Mr. Moenter says, "I went up to get our licenses and there, by gosh, was our barn."

Author's Note: The above article was reprinted from the Delphos, Ohio, *Daily Herald* in its entirety. A photograph of the barn which was contemporary with the article is no long available. Sometime between 1974 and 1976 the barn was torn down.

Appendix D: Resume of Frederick John Kunz

In the early nineteen hundreds Putnam County, Ohio, workers erected an iron bridge across the Auglaize River about a half mile from the Kunz homestead. An iron medallion affixed at the bridge's uppermost beam indicated that the bridge was built in 1905. As a child Frederick was told by his parents that the bridge was built the year he was born. (Apparently, no birth certificate for Frederick was filed in Putnam County by the doctor/midwife or his parents.) When he was baptized into the Catholic Church, his mother and sisters declared he was born in 1906. This dilemma was never resolved and caused considerable difficulty when Frederick sought Social Security in the late nineteen sixties. During his work years this legal uncertainty was of no consequence to Frederick as he consistently stuck "to the bridge's story." It does point out, however, that from the very first his extraordinary creative will and clear memory would serve him well for all of his 69, or 68, years.

It is quite possible that Frederick never wrote a resume. It appears he was always known by his work and would be sought out by persons who needed his design and inventive capabilities. His formal training consisted of an apprenticeship with his master carpenter father Ferdinand, a home study course in mechanical drafting, intensive self-study of mathematics, and an apprenticeship with B. J. Gramm, originator of the Liberty truck. For all else he depended on his innate ability to visualize design problems and solve them whether they were related to a semi-trailer, voting machine or commercial architectural construction. Frederick Kunz was, in every sense of the phrase, a Renaissance man.

Each person who knew Frederick knew him in a different way; some knew him as a devoted naturalist raising acres of trees and flowers, others saw his lapidary and jewelry making skills. Still others knew him for his architectural home design and interior furnishings. More still knew him for his love of American Indian lore and firsthand knowledge of Indian objects he found along the Auglaize River. He could paint a first-rate watercolor as easily as he could help a friend design a workable farm truck or machine part. He seldom took payment from anyone he assisted, seeming instead to take

151

satisfaction from just having "solved" the problem. He kept his "secret" Perpetual Motion machine parts under his bed or hidden in the basement away from prying eyes. (It was a dream that he, like many of his generation, would never give up on.) From time to time he would invent and copyright a little household product like a stainless steel condensed milk can top that automatically punched two holes in the milk can lid then remained in place to seal it. Another favorite was an ingenious cap for soda bottles that sealed them and kept "the fizz" in.

His quiet joy in life was reading the *National Geographic Magazine*. Every evening there was time set aside for quiet reading. He could talk for hours about countries he had "traveled to." In actuality he traveled very little outside the confines of western Ohio and eastern Indiana. One trip to the West in 1946 and two trips to the East in later years served to suffice for "actual" travel. A heavy work schedule and a growing family to support and provide for were sufficient reasons to live life as Henry David Thoreau suggested, "getting to know one's own doorstep."

Below is a brief chronology of Frederick's work years, drawn from the memories of family members.

1917-1921	Worked with father building home and barns in the Delphos/ Fort Jennings, Ohio, area.
1921-1925	Ran his own auto mechanics garage in Delphos, Ohio.
1925-1928	Apprenticed with B.J. Gramm Company of Delphos, Ohio, in mechanical drawing.
1928-1932	Worked in truck design department at International Harvester in Fort Wayne, Indiana. (Lost position in 1932 because of Depression.)
1932-1935	Worked as day laborer and house/barn painter in Delphos/Fort Jennings, Ohio, area.
1935-1941	Regained position in specialized vehicle design at International Harvester.

1941- 1958	Returned to B. J. Gramm in Delphos, Ohio, to design special vehicles for the US Army. Designed military post office van and milk carrier along with other specialized trucks. Invented the FIVE CAR CARRIER which transported autos to a destination then folded to a flat bed for transport of various materials on return trip. The CARRIER and other inventions created by Frederick were owned and held under the copyright of the Gramm/Fruehauf Company.
Late 1950s	Frederick suffered a massive heart attack in the late 1950s. After a long period of recuperation, choosing not to go back to the "drawing board" immediately, he spent a year or so doing inside finish wood work on structures being built by his nephew and protégée Richard Osting, of Delphos, Ohio.
1960- 1962	Worked in the tool and die division of Lennox Industries in Lima, Ohio. Among his projects at Lennox were the machine that made Gaines Burgers for dogs and a new simplified voting machine.
1962- 1972	Worked for Wolf Industries, Lima, Ohio, as their chief architectural designer. While there he designed and supervised the building of almost thirty large nursing homes in Ohio. This pioneer effort established Frederick as a valuable resource in Ohio for the design and construction of elderly care facilities.

Two years after his retirement, Frederick was busy re-doing the kitchen and other home projects and planning for a long fishing trip. He had constructed a small wooden trailer to hitch to his auto to hold all his fishing essentials for a week's stay. The night before he was to have left, he passed away peacefully in his sleep, leaving all who knew him to remember Frederick as they had known him. True to his memory, his obituaries and his grave marker state that he was born in 1905.

Pedigree Chart

The following Pedigree Chart was assembled and prepared by Carol and Ronald Kunz from research done over a period of more than twenty years. The Chart traces the Kunz/Lause bloodline from its earliest beginnings in America in 1640 to the marriage of Frederick Kunz and Viola Lause in 1929.

My deepest thanks are extended to Carol and Ronald Kunz for their sustained efforts on behalf of our families.

Pedigree Chart

FIRST GENERATION

1. **Winona Marie Kunz** was born in Fort Wayne, Indiana to Frederick John Kunz and Viola Mary Lause.

SECOND GENERATION

2. **Frederick John Kunz** was born on October 4, 1905 to Frederick Kunz and Deflora Alice "Flo" Clawson in Fort Jennings, Putnam County, Ohio. He was christened on May 10, 1913 in St. John the Evangelist Catholic Church, Delphos, Ohio. Frederick married Viola Mary Lause on November 19, 1929 at St. Patrick Catholic Church in Fort Wayne, Indiana. Fred was a retired draftsman for Wolfe Industries. He died on July 27, 1974 at his residence in Fort Jennings, Ohio. He was buried on July 30, 1974 in Delphos St. John's Cemetery, Section W-S, Lot 31, Grave 2.
Cause of Death: Heart Attack.

Obituary Delphos Herald July 1974:

DELPHOS - Frederick J. Kunz, 68, of Rt. 2, Fort Jennings died at 3 a.m. Saturday in his residence. Born in Fort Jennings Oct. 4, 1905, he was the son of Frederick and Flo Clawson Kunz. He was married in 1929 to Viola Mary Lause, who survives.

Also surviving are two daughters, Mrs. Winona Garmhausen of Santa Fe, N.M., and Mrs. William (Sylvia) Vest of Lima; four sons, Steven at home, Norman and Ronald of Delphos, and Larry of Lima; two sisters, Mrs. Eva Osting of here and Edith Kunz of Lima; and 18 grandchildren.

He was a member of St. John's Catholic Church, where Mass of the Resurrection will be held 10 a.m. Tuesday. Burial will be in the church cemetery.

Friends may call after 7 p.m. today at Kolkmeyer-Helmkamp Funeral Home, where Parish Wake services will be held at 8 p.m. Monday.

3. **Viola Mary Lause** was born on February 4, 1909 in Delphos, Ohio to Frederick J. Lause II and Helena Maria "Lena" Moreo. She was christened on February 7, 1909 in Delphos St. John the Evangelist Catholic Church. Viola married Frederick John Kunz on November 19, 1929 at St. Patrick Catholic Church in Fort Wayne, Indiana. She resided in Fort Jennings, Ohio.

Frederick John Kunz and Viola Mary Lause had the following children:

a. **Winona Marie Kunz. (# 1 on chart)**

b. **Norman John Kunz** was born on March 16, 1932 in Fort Jennings, Ohio. He died on August 27, 1993 in Columbus, Ohio.

c. **Sylvia Ann Kunz.**

d. **Ronald Joseph Kunz.**

e. **Larry David Kunz.**

f. **Steven Michael Kunz.**

THIRD GENERATION

4. **Frederick Kunz** was born on November 6, 1860 in Dayton, Ohio to Franz Michael Kunz and Margaretha Marz. Frederick was married to Deflora Alice "Flo" Clawson September 6, 1890 in Allen County, Ohio by D. E. Baxter J.P. Their marriage was validated November 22, 1913 at Delphos St. John the Evangelist Catholic Church by Rev. F. Rupert. Frederick was a Carpenter. He died on March 1, 1932 in Fort Jennings, Ohio at the age of 71 years. He was buried on March 4, 1932 in Delphos St. John's Cemetery, Section O, Lot 18, Grave 4. AKA: Ferdinand Kunz.

Obituary Delphos Herald March 1932:
FREDERICK KUNZ PASSES AWAY EARLY TUESDAY
   A well-known resident of four and one-half miles northeast of Delphos, Frederick Kunz, succumbed at his home Tuesday morning at 4:45 o'clock. His death followed a serious illness of two weeks and was caused by a catarrhal infection.
   Mr. Kunz was born at Dayton on November 6, 1860. Forty-one years ago, he was united in marriage to Miss Flora Clawson. There were three children born to this union.
   For years, Mr. Kunz was engaged in the carpenter trade. He resided in this vicinity for the past fifty years. When his death occurred, he was seventy-one years, three months and twenty-four days of age. He was a member of St. John's Catholic Church.
   Besides his widow, he is survived by: two daughters, Mrs. Ben Osting, east of Delphos; and Miss Edith Kunz of Lima; and one son, Frederick Kunz, at home. There are six grandchildren and one brother, Frank Kunz, East Fourth Street, also survives.
   Funeral services will be held at St. John's Catholic Church Friday morning at 9:30 o'clock. Interment will be made at St. John's Cemetery.
   Last rites for Frederick Kunz were conducted at St. John's Catholic Church. The requiem high mass was intoned by Rev. Father Mehling and Monsignor F. Rupert delivered the sermon. The following officiated as pallbearers: Andrew Saum, John Saum,

Herman Mericle, Theodore Hageman, Ferd Eggeman, and George Hunsaker.

5. **Deflora Alice "Flo" Clawson** was born on May 25, 1873 in Delphos, Ohio to Josiah Clawson and Malinda Emily Hartshorn. She was married to Frederick Kunz September 6, 1890 in Allen County, Ohio by D. E. Baxter J.P. Marriage was validated November 22, 1913 at Delphos St. John the Evangelist Catholic Church by Rev. F. Rupert. She was christened on November 22, 1913 in St. John the Evangelist Catholic Church, Delphos, Ohio by Rev. F. Rupert. She died on September 27, 1943 in Delphos, Ohio. She was buried on September 30, 1943 in Delphos St. John's Cemetery, Section O, Lot 20, Grave 3. Cause of Death: Stroke (70 years).

Obituary Delphos Herald September 1943:
DEATH OF MRS. FLORA KUNZ

Mrs. Flora A. Kunz, a lifelong resident of this community, died at her home at 917 East Second Street at 11:00 o'clock Monday evening. On Friday of last week, she suffered a stroke and since that time, her condition had been serious.

Born near Delphos on May 25, 1873, Flora Clawson was a daughter of Josiah and Malinda Clawson. Her marriage to Fred Kunz took place on September 6, 1890. The death of Mr. Kunz occurred on March 1, 1932. Three years ago, Mrs. Kunz moved from her home northeast of this city to East Second street.

When her death occurred, she was seventy years, four months and two days of age. She was a member of St. John's Church, the Altar Society and the Sacred Heart League.

Surviving are: two daughters and a son, Mrs. Ben Osting, northeast of Delphos; Miss Edith Kunz, at home; and Frederick Kunz, northeast of Delphos; nine grandchildren; one great-grandchild; five sisters, Mrs. Glen Fosnaugh, Lacombe, Alberta, Canada; Mrs. Nellie Allen, Detroit; and Mrs. Cleo Louth, Mrs. Bessie Bly and Miss Fanny Clawson, of Lima; and a brother, Harry Clawson, East Fifth street. She was preceded in death in 1918 by a brother, Roy Clawson.

A grandson, Arnold Osting, Camp Parks, California, is with the United States Navy.

Services will be conducted at St. John's church at 9:00 o'clock Thursday morning. Interment will be in the church cemetery. The remains will be at the Jaumann-Kolkmeyer funeral home until the time of the services.

Frederick Kunz and Deflora Alice "Flo" Clawson had the following children:

    a. **Eva M. Kunz** was born on July 26, 1894 in Fort Jennings, Ohio. She was christened on May 11, 1912 in St. John the Evangelist Catholic Church, Delphos, Ohio. She married Bernard H. Osting October 15, 1913 at St. John the Evangelist Catholic Church in Delphos, Ohio. (Bernard was born August 19, 1888 and died December 25, 1952.) Eva died at the age of 84 years on May 15, 1979 at the Delphos Memorial Nursing Home in Delphos, Ohio. She was buried on May 18, 1979 in Delphos St. John's Cemetery, Section K, Lot 5.

    b. **Edith K. Kunz** was born on May 25, 1900 in Fort Jennings, Ohio. She was christened on May 10, 1913 in St. John the Evangelist Catholic Church, Delphos, Ohio. She resided in Lima, Ohio. She was retired from Ottawa Valley Hospital and had worked for Myers Cleaners. Edith never married. She had diabetes for many years. She died on August 8, 1981 at Lima Manor Nursing Home in Lima, Ohio at the age of 81 years. She was buried on August 10, 1981 in Delphos St. John's Cemetery, Section O, Lot 19, Grave 9.

    c. **Frederick John Kunz (# 2 on chart)** was born on October 4, 1905. He was married to Viola Mary Lause.

6. **Frederick J. Lause II** was born on December 29, 1875 in Delphos, Ohio to Frederick J. Lause and Mary A. Pohlman. He married Helena Maria "Lena" Moreo on October 24, 1900 at St. John the Evangelist Catholic Church in Delphos, Ohio. He was a Farmer and resided in Delphos, Ohio. He died on May 3, 1954 in Delphos, Ohio. He was buried on May 6, 1954 in Delphos St. John's Cemetery, Section A, Lot 24, Grave 4.
Cause of Death: Myocarditis, Rheumatism, Influenza.

Obituary Delphos Herald May 4, 1954:
FRED LAUSE DIES MONDAY
Death of Local Farmer Occurs Following Day's Serious Illness.
Widow, Eleven Children Survive.
Funeral Mass Thursday at St. John's Catholic Church.
Burial in Church Cemetery.

Fred J. Lause died at 2:00 p.m. Monday, May 3, 1954, at his home south of Delphos, following a serious illness of one day.

He was born December 29, 1875 in Delphos, the son of Frederick and Mary Lause. At the time of his death he was 78 years, 4 months and 4 days of age.

On October 24, 1900, he was married at St. John's Catholic church, Delphos, to Miss Lena Moreo.

Mrs. Lause still survives, as do the following children: George Lause, Delphos, Mrs. Lucille Crede, Delphos, Frank Lause, Detroit, Mrs. Viola Kunz, Ft. Jennings, Mrs. Coletta Metcalfe, Lafayette, Indiana, Ralph Lause, Eugene Lause and Norval Lause, Delphos, Harold Lause, Van Wert, and Ernest and Donald Lause, Delphos; 24 grandchildren; 1 great grandchild; one sister, Mrs. Clara Moore, Everett, Washington; and two brothers, Clem and A. W. both of Delphos. One son, Herbert, preceded him in death.

A farmer, he was a member of St. John's Catholic church in this city.

Funeral mass will be intoned at 9:00 a.m. Thursday at St. John's Catholic church. Burial will be made in the church cemetery.

The remains will be at the Oscar A. Kolkmeyer funeral home where friends may call until time for the services.

7. **Helena Maria "Lena" Moreo** was born on September 13, 1882 in Landeck, Ohio to Andrew Moreo and Christina Caroline Loy. She married Frederick J. Lause II on October 24, 1900 at St. John the Evangelist Catholic Church in Delphos, Ohio. She died on May 20, 1967 in Delphos, Ohio. She was buried on May 23, 1967 in Delphos St. John's Cemetery, Section A, Lot 24, Grave 6.

Obituary Delphos Herald May 1967:
LENA LAUSE
DELPHOS – Mrs. Lena Lause, 84, of 549 Toomey Ave. died at 9:15 a.m. Saturday in the Del-Ward Nursing Center following a one year

illness. Born Sept. 13, 1882 in Landeck, she was the daughter of Andrew and Christine Loy Moreo. In 1900 she was married here to Fred J. Lause, who died May 3, 1954.

She was a member of the St. John's Catholic Church, the Rosary Alter Society and the Sacred Heart League.

Survivors include three daughters, Mrs. Harry (Lucille) Crede of Delphos, Mrs. Fred (Viola) Kunz of Fort Jennings, Mrs. Howard (Coletta) Metcalf of West Lafayette, Indiana; seven sons, Frank of Roseville, Michigan, Eugene of Landeck, Harold of Fort Myers, Florida, Ralph, Norval, George, Ernest and Donald, all of Delphos; 28 grandchildren and 20 great-grandchildren; a brother, John Moreo, of Perrysburg and two sisters, Mrs. Susan Lucius of Delphos, and Mrs. Mary Vogt of Cridersville.

Requiem High Mass will be offered at 9:30 a.m. Tuesday in the Church, Rev. Joseph Schill officiating, with burial in the church cemetery. Friends may call at the Kolkmeyer Funeral Home after two this afternoon.

Frederick J. Lause II and Helena Maria "Lena" Moreo had the following children:

> a. **George A. Lause** was born on March 31, 1904 in Delphos, Ohio. He was a farmer. He married Rose M. Hotz on August 24, 1926. (Rose born August 27, 1904 and died December 29, 1989.) George died on December 11, 1980 in Delphos, Ohio at the age of 76 years. He was buried on December 13, 1980 in Delphos St. John's Resurrection Cemetery, Section A-3, Lot 29. Cause of Death: Heart Attack.

> b. **Lucille Ethel Lause** was born on December 20, 1905 in Delphos, Ohio. She married Eugene Lewis Irvin on October 7, 1924. (Eugene died February 1940.) In 1951 she married Harry A. Crede, Jr. (Harry born February 20, 1922 and died June 5, 1996.) Lucille died on February 12, 1973 in Fort Myers, Florida in an auto accident. She was buried on February 17, 1973 in Delphos Walnut Grove Cemetery, Highway Section.

c. **Frank O. Lause** was born on October 18, 1907 in Delphos, Ohio. He married Helen Ostendorf on August 30, 1941. He resided in Roseville, Michigan. He was a Factory Worker. Frank died on April 28, 1971 in Roseville, Michigan. He was buried in Roseville Resurrection Cemetery. Cause of Death: Cancer of the Brain.

d. **Viola Mary Lause (# 3 on chart)** was born on February 4, 1909. She was married to Frederick John Kunz.

e. **Coletta Susan Lause** was born on June 10, 1910 in Delphos, Ohio. She married Calvin J. Freund on September 9, 1931. They were divorced. She married Howard A. Metcalfe DDS on March 15, 1941. (Howard born December 4, 1911 and died September 18, 1966.) Coletta died on February 12, 1973 in Fort Myers, Florida in an auto accident. She was buried on February 17, 1973 in Delphos St. John's Cemetery, Section X, Lot 2, Grave 4.

f. **Ralph Clem Lause** was born on November 7, 1911 in Delphos, Ohio. He married Esther Bertha Vogt on January 2, 1937 in Delphos, Ohio. (Esther born October 11, 1917 and died October 6, 2003.) He was a Factory Worker. Ralph died on January 1, 1986 in Delphos, Ohio. He was buried on January 4, 1986 in Delphos St. John's Resurrection Cemetery, Section A-2, Lot 23. Cause of Death: Cancer.

g. **Eugene J. "Ike" Lause** was born on November 8, 1913 in Delphos, Ohio. He married Margaret Suever on June 29, 1939 in Landeck, Ohio. He resided in Landeck, Ohio. He was retired from Suever Stone Company and a Farmer. Eugene died on September 7, 1985 at St. Rita's Hospital in Lima, Ohio. He was buried on September 9, 1985 in Landeck St. John the Baptist Cemetery. Cause of Death: Cancer.

h. **Herbert L. Lause** was born on November 18, 1916 in Delphos, Ohio. He died on February 23, 1917 in Delphos, Ohio at the age of 3 months. He was buried on February

25, 1917 in Delphos St. John's Cemetery, Section A, Lot 24, Grave 2. Cause of Death: Meningitis.

i. **Norval L.F. "Bunny" Lause** was born on July 25, 1918 in Delphos, Ohio. He married Pauline R. Schwinnen on October 9, 1943 in Delphos, Ohio. He was a retired owner-operator of the Star Cafe and the Phelan Hotel. Norval died on May 2, 1989 in Delphos, Ohio. He was buried on May 5, 1989 in Delphos St. John's Resurrection Cemetery, Section A-2, Lot 88. Cause of Death: Cancer.

j. **Harold J. "Fritz" Lause** was born on June 30, 1920 in Delphos, Ohio. He married Hope Fox on February 25, 1941 at Delphos, Ohio. He resided in Fort Myers, Florida. He was the Founder of Golf Paving at Fort Myers, Florida. Harold died on February 7, 1984 in Fort Myers, Florida. He was buried in Fort Myers Memorial Gardens Cemetery. Cause of Death: Stroke.

k. **Ernest Charles Lause** was born on July 5, 1922 in Delphos, Ohio. He married Mary Margaret Schwinnen on February 13, 1943. He was the owner-operator of the Rustic Cafe in Delphos. He was a U.S. Navy World War II Veteran. Ernest died on December 24, 1978 in Delphos, Ohio. He was buried on December 28, 1978 in Delphos St. John's Cemetery, Section Z, Grave 91. Cause of Death: Cancer.

l. **Donald Glen Lause** was born on December 16, 1923 in Delphos, Ohio. He married Eileen A. Suever on January 20, 1948 in Delphos, Ohio. He was a Co-owner of Suever Stone Company. Donald died on January 31, 1990 in Delphos, Ohio. He was buried on February 3, 1990 in Delphos St. John's Resurrection Cemetery, Section L-1, Lot 57D. Cause of Death: Heart Attack.

FOURTH GENERATION

8. Franz Michael Kunz was born on May 22, 1819 in Rheinzabern, Bavaria, Germany to Franz Anton Kunz and Margaretha Feinholz. He married Margaretha Marz on May 10, 1847 in Rheinzabern, Germany. He was a Farmer. He died on January 26, 1890 in Delphos, Ohio. He was buried on January 28, 1890 in Delphos St. John's Cemetery.

AKA: Francis Kunz, Frank Kunz and surname misspelled as Kuntz.

Source: Register office of Rheinzabern Birth entry Nr.29
(Per Reinhard Hofer, Ruhstorf, Germany, genealogy researcher in Germany)

Kunz Franz Michael d.o.b. 22.5.1819

Franz Anton Kunz, 33 years of age, farmer, residing in Rheinzabern, county of Candel, court of Germersheim, district of Rhine, Kingdom of Bavaria, declares before the officer of Rheinzabern, that on May 22nd of 1819 at 6 o'clock a.m., a son was born by his wife Margaretha Feinholz, who is named Franz Michael.

Witnesses: Franz Michael Thomas, 39 years. Andreas Tentschler, 31 years. Both day workers at Rheinzabern.

Signatures: Kunz (hand sign) declared that he is unable to write, Thomas, Tentschler.

Source: Register office of Rheinzabern Marriage entry 1847 Nr.6
Kunz Franz Michael and Marz Margaretha

Groom Franz Michael Kunz, d.o.b. on 22nd of May 1819 in Rheinzabern, of occupation a day worker, residing at Rheinzabern, county Candel, department of Landau in der Pfalz, Kingdom of Bavaria celebrates in front of the officer mayor of Rheinzabern, Johann Adam Orth, wedding on 10th of May, 1847.

Parents of groom: Franz Anton Kunz d.o.d. on 11th February 1844 and wife Margaretha Feinholz d.o.d. on 15th December 1836.

Grandparents on father's side: Jacob Kunz d.o.d. on 15th January 1794 and wife Margaretha Franzoni d.o.d. on 17th February 1819.

Grandparents on mother's side: Bonifaz Feinholz d.o.d. on 15th Sept. 1834 and wife Elizabeth Reihs d.o.d. on 18th April 1830.

The above given dates are all registered at the office of Rheinzabern. Groom shows evidence of his quitting military on March 11th of 1847, dated in Landau in der Pfalz, of the Royal Bavarian Infantry Regiment "Herzog Wilhelm".

The mayor declares that groom Kunz has sworn his oath of a citizen in Rheinzabern.

Franz Michael Kunz, also known as Francis Kunz and Frank Kunz, came to America on the Ship "LISBON" from LeHavre (Northern France) to New York with his wife and 4 children. They arrived May 29, 1854 and settled at Dayton, Ohio. In 1865 he moved to Van Wert, Ohio, and after spending eight years there, moved to Allen County, Ohio in 1873. Mr. Kunz purchased a farm from James Kiggins on Kiggins Road on land contract. Mr. Kunz appears in the 1860 Montgomery County, Harrison Twp, Dayton, Ohio census and also 1870 census of Van Wert County, York Twp, Van Wert, Ohio. In 1860 census he was shown as 41 years old and from Bavaria, in 1870 listed as from Prussia, 50 years old and a Farmer. The 1882 Beers, History of Montgomery County, Ohio (page 432) states he had served 6 years in the German Regular Army before coming to America. Allen County Probate (Death Record Book #2, page 138) gives death date as Feb. 2, 1890. Delphos St. John's Church death records state Franz died Jan. 26, 1890 and buried Jan. 28, 1890, Father A. I. Hoeffel as priest. Age 71 years old. Franz's memorial stone in St. John's Cemetery is missing.

Obituary Delphos Herald January 30, 1890:

Frank Kuntz, a well-known farmer living two miles south-east of this place, died last Saturday night, aged 71 years. The funeral services were held at St. John's church Tuesday morning. Mr. Kuntz was an upright, conscientious man, warmly liked by his neighbors, and his family has the sympathy of a large circle of friends in their sad loss.

9. **Margaretha Marz** was born on April 3, 1819 in Rheinzabern, Bavaria, Germany to Franz Michael Marz and Maria Anna Himmelsbach. She married Franz Michael Kunz on May 10, 1847 in Rheinzabern, Germany. She died on September 1, 1892 in Delphos,

Ohio. She was buried on September 3, 1892 in Delphos St. John's Cemetery.

AKA: Margaretha Martz and Margaret Martz.

Source: Register office of Rheinzabern Birth entry 1819 Nr.20
(Per Reinhard Hofer, genealogy researcher in Germany)
Marz Margaretha d.o.b. 3.April.1819

Franz Michael Marz, the younger, 41 years of age, of occupation a farmer, residing in Rheinzabern, County of Candel, District of Germersheim, Royal Bavarian Rheinkreis, declares in front of the officer mayor of Rheinzabern, that on April 3rd of 1819 at 9 o'clock in the morning, his wife Maria Anna Himmelsbach, gave birth to a daughter, named Margaretha.

Witnesses: Philipp Jacob Reib, 35 years, farmer. Anton Geldmann, 47 years, locksmith. Both residing in Rheinzabern.
Signatures: Marz, Geldmann, Reib, Officer Topper.

Source: Register office of Rheinzabern Marriage Entry 1847 Nr.6
Kunz Franz Michael and Marz Margaretha

Bride Margaretha, maiden name Marz, of no occupation, d.o.b. on 3rd of April 1819 in Rheinzabern. Accompanied with her 79 year old father, Franz Michael Marz, a farmer being present and willing with the wedding. Her mother has been Maria Anna Himmelsbach d.o.d. on 4th of December 1829.

The above given deaths are all registered at the office of Rheinzabern.

Delphos St. John's death records show Margaretha died at 75 years of age on Sept. 1, 1892 and buried Sept. 3, 1892, Father Q. B. Heiland as priest. She came to America on ship LISBON with her husband, Franz and 4 children on May 29, 1854.

Franz Michael Kunz and Margaretha Marz had the following children:

    a. **Joseph Kunz** was born on March 2, 1848 in Rheinzabern, Bavaria, Germany. He married Sarah E. Armstrong in Dayton, Ohio on May 4, 1871. Joseph resided in Dayton, Ohio and he was a Gardener at the Dayton State Hospital. Joseph died on November 20, 1927 in Dayton, Ohio. He was buried on November 23, 1927 in Dayton Greencastle Cemetery.

Source: Register office of Rheinzabern Birth entry Nr.10
(Per Reinhard Hofer, genealogy researcher in Germany)
Kunz Joseph d.o.b. 2.Marz.1848 at 4 p.m.
Rheinzabern, county of Kandel, district Landau in der Pfalz, Kingdom of Bavaria, Franz Michael Kunz, 28 years of age, married, occupation a farmer, residing in Rheinzabern, declares on March 2nd, of 1848 at 4 o'clock p.m. a male child was born by his wife Margaretha Marz, 28 years, of no occupation, residing with him, who will be named Joseph.

Witnesses: Franz Klein, 75 years, no occupation. Johann Adam Seither, 35 years, farmer. Both of Rheinzabern.
Signatures: Kunz, Klein, Seither.

Montgomery Co, Harrison Twp, Ohio 1880 Census:
Joseph 32yrs, Sarah 33yrs, Frank 8yrs, Harry 6yrs, Blanche 3yrs, Edney 7 months.

Joseph Kunz, gardener, P.O. Dayton, was born in Germany March 2, 1848 according to the 1882 Beers Biographical Sketch. Joseph came to America with his parents on the Ship Lisbon May 29, 1854. Joseph stayed with his parents until nineteen years of age, when he commenced work as a gardener. At age 22, he married Sarah Armstrong of near Sandusky, Ohio, and they had five children, four now living (1882). They were all members of the United Brethren Church, of which Joseph was a Steward.

Funeral Rites - The Dayton Daily News Nov. 21, 1927:
JOSEPH KUNZ
Funeral of Joseph Kunz, who died Sunday at his residence, 1834 Arbor Ave., will be held at the residence at 2 p.m. Wednesday. Burial will be in Greencastle cemetery. He had lived in Dayton for years. He leaves two sons, Frank

and Harry Kunz, two daughters, seventeen grandchildren and seven great grandchildren.

Greencastle cemetery is located just West of I-75 on Edwin C. Moses Ave. There are two Greencastle cemeteries, Old and New. Joseph is buried in the old cemetery which was located next to his church. In the cemetery, his stone is near the church along with his wife Sarah, a small stone for Hattie J. Kunz, d/o J. and S. Kunz, age 3y 8m 8d, died Nov. 16, 1878 and another stone J. Vernon Kunz, 1884 - 1918.

b. **George Anthony Kunz** was born on September 16, 1849 in Rheinzabern, Bavaria, Germany. He married Margaret "Maggie" Bentley in Dayton, Ohio on November 12, 1874. He resided in Dayton, Ohio and Fayetteville, Arkansas. He was a Gardener. George died on August 10, 1930 in Fayetteville, Arkansas. He was buried on August 13, 1930 in Fayetteville Evergreen Cemetery.

Source: Register office of Rheinzabern Birth entry Nr.62
(Per Reinhard Hofer, genealogy researcher in Germany)
   <u>**Kunz Georg Anton d.o.b. 16.9.1849 at 4 p.m.**</u>
Franz Michael Kunz, 30 years of age, married, occupation a day worker, residing in Rheinzabern, county of Kandel, district Landau in der Pfalz, Kingdom of Bavaria, declares on 16th of September 1849 at 7 p.m., before the officer Jacob Weigel of Rheinzabern, that today at 4 o'clock p.m., a male child was born by his wife Margaretha Marz, 30 years, of no occupation, residing with him, who will be named Georg Anton.

Witnesses: Sebastian Kunz, 44 years. Franz Peter Kunz, 39 years. Both day workers of Rheinzabern.
Signatures: Kunz, Kunz, Kunz.

Montgomery Co, Harrison Twp, Ohio 1880 Census:
Geo A. 30yrs, Margaret 31yrs, Edwin 4yrs, Eliza 3yrs, Sarah 2yrs, Elnorea 2½yrs.

George A. Kunz, gardener, P.O. Dayton, a brother of Joseph Kunz, was born in Germany, September, 1849 according to 1882 Beers Biographical Sketch. George came to America with his parents on the Ship Lisbon May 29, 1854. Until of age, he lived with his parents helping in the garden and going to school. He began life for himself as a gardener and continued in this same employment. George married in 1874 to Maggie Bentley, whose parents came from Maryland at an early day, and settled in Harrison Township. George and Maggie had four children and all were members of the First Lutheran Church. George was also connected with Patterson Chapel Sabbath School from its organization, and from 1875 had been its Treasurer.

Obituary Fayetteville Daily Democrat August 11, 1930: GEORGE A. KUNZ PASSES AWAY

George Anthony Kunz, nearly 81, died suddenly at his home on Cleveland Avenue Sunday evening about 5:30 o'clock. He had been eating supper when the end came. Funeral arrangements are not complete awaiting further word from his son, Elmer Kunz of Denver, Colorado.

Native of Bavaria

Mr. Kunz was born in Bavaria, September 16, 1849. He came with his parents to America when he was three years old. He was married at Dayton, Ohio to Miss Margaret Bentley who died August 18, 1921. About 30 years ago he came to Fayetteville and for 17 years was foreman in the horticultural department at the University of Arkansas. Mr. Kunz was considered the best informed and most successful market gardener in this part of the state. He was a member of the Central Presbyterian church in which for many years he was an elder.

Leaves Seven Children

Surviving are five daughters and two sons: Miss Lida Kunz, who made a home for her father after the mother's death; Mrs. R. J. Crabill of Allen, Oklahoma; Mrs. M. L. Gillespie of Little Rock; Mrs. V. N. Gregg of Plainfield, New Jersey; Mrs. C. T. Brown of Little Rock; Elmer Kunz of Denver and Clifford Kunz of Okmulgee, Oklahoma. All except Mrs. Brown, who visited here last week and now is in New York, are expected for the funeral services.

Fayetteville Daily Democrat August 12, 1930:
GEORGE A. KUNZ Funeral Here Wednesday at 4

Funeral services for George Anthony Kunz, who died suddenly at his home on Cleveland Avenue Sunday evening will be held Wednesday afternoon at four o'clock in Central Presbyterian church. Burial will be at the Evergreen Cemetery. Rev. M. L. Gillespie and Rev. H. G. Finney will have charge with Mildred Gillespie at the organ.

Pallbearers are Joe Bates, Steve Bates, J. E. Dowell, F. P. Earle, C. A. Marshall and Dr. Harrison Hale.

Elmer Kunz of Denver, a son of the deceased has not yet arrived but is expected tonight or tomorrow morning.

Fayetteville Daily Democrat August 14, 1930:
GEORGE A. KUNZ IS LAID TO REST

Funeral services were held yesterday at the Central Presbyterian church for George A. Kunz, who passed away Sunday evening. His son-in-law, Rev. M. L. Gillespie of Little Rock and his pastor, Rev. H. G. Finney, officiated. Interment was in Evergreen cemetery.

A quartette composed of Captain Guy A. Kinman, Mrs. Felix Spencer, Miss Hazel Johnson and Dr. D. M. Moore, sang two hymns, "Rock of Ages," and "Save in the Arms of Jesus," accompanied on the organ by Miss Mildred Gillespie.

c. **Elizabeth Kunz** was born on December 5, 1850 in Rheinzabern, Bavaria, Germany. Elizabeth came to America with her parents on the Ship Lisbon May 29, 1854. She married Henry Michael Hager July 17, 1877 in Dayton, Ohio. (Henry born June 25, 1851 and died March 17, 1925.) Elizabeth died on November 21, 1926 in Dayton, Montgomery County, Ohio. She was buried on November 24, 1926 in Memorial Park, Dayton, Ohio.

Cause of Death: Senility.
Sources: Death Certificate; A History of David Hager and his Descendants by Margot Allred Hager.

Source: Register office of Rheinzabern Birth entry 1850 Nr.10
(Per Reinhard Hofer, genealogy researcher in Germany)
Kunz Elizabetha d.o.b. 5.12.1850 at 6 a.m.
Franz Michael Kunz, 31 years of age, occupation a farmer, residing at Rheinzabern, county of Candel, department of Landau in der Pfalz, Kingdom of Bavaria, declares in front of the officer mayor of Rheinzabern, Jacob Weigel, that on December 5th, 1850 at 6 o'clock in the morning, his wife Margaretha, maiden name Marz, of no occupation, gave birth to a daughter, named Elisabetha.

Witnesses: Nikolaus Feinholz, 41 years, barrel maker. Sebastian Kunz, 45 years, day worker. Both residing at Rheinzabern.
Signatures: Kunz, Feinholz, Kunz.

d. **Barbara Kunz** was born on April 20, 1853 in Rheinzabern, Bavaria, Germany. She came to America with her parents on the Ship Lisbon May 29, 1854. She died on July 5, 1865 in Delphos, Ohio at the age of 12 years. She was buried on July 6, 1865 in Delphos St. John's OLD Cemetery, Section A, Row 10, Grave 110.

Source: Register office of Rheinzabern Birth entry 1853 Nr.16
(Per Reinhard Hofer, Genealogy researcher in Germany)
Kunz Barbara d.o.b. 20.4.1853 at 9 p.m.
Franz Michael Kunz, 33 years of age, occupation a day worker, residing at Rheinzabern, county Candel, department of Landau in der Pfalz, Kingdom of Bavaria, declares in front of the officer mayor of Rheinzabern, Jacob Weigel, that on April 20th of 1853 at 9 o'clock at night, his wife Margaretha, maiden name Marz, of no occupation, gave birth to a daughter, named Barbara.

Witnesses: Franz Michael Feinholz, 56 years, officer and farmer. Phillipp Jacob Hamburger, 46 years, police servant. Both residing at Rheinzabern.
Signatures: Kunz, Feinholz, Hamburger.

e. **Mary Kunz** was born on September 9, 1858 in Dayton, Ohio. She died on June 23, 1916 at 208 E. Cleveland Street, Delphos, Ohio. She was buried on June 26, 1916 in Delphos St. John's Cemetery, Section B, Lot 7, Grave 3. Cause of Death: Cancer of Uterus.

f. **Frederick Kunz (# 4 on chart)** was born on November 6, 1860. He was married to Deflora Alice "Flo" Clawson.

g. **Philabena Kunz** was born on July 12, 1862 in Dayton, Ohio. She married Marion Thurston February 17, 1897 in Lima, Ohio. Philabena died on March 23, 1928 in Delphos, Ohio. She was buried on March 26, 1928 in Delphos St. John's Cemetery, Section B, Lot 13, Grave 3. Cause of Death: Carcinoma of Uterus.
Source: Death Certificate.

Obituary Delphos Herald March 1928:
MRS. THURSTON PASSES AWAY FRIDAY A.M.

Mrs. Philabena Thurston passed away at her home on East Cleveland Street, Friday morning at 7:45 o'clock. She had been in failing health for some time prior to her death, although her condition was not considered serious until about two weeks ago. Her death was due to complications. She was 65 years, 8 months and 11 days of age at the time her death occurred.

Miss Kunz was the daughter of Frank and Margarite Kunz and was born July 12, 1862 at Montgomery County, near Dayton, Ohio. She was united in marriage to Marion Thurston at Lima, he having preceded her in death in 1913. She was a resident of this city for the past twenty-seven years and is well known here. She has a host of friends who will be sorry to learn of her death. No children were born to Mr. and Mrs. Thurston.

Surviving to mourn her death are three brothers, George Kunz, of Fayetteville, Ark.; Frederick Kunz, east of Delphos, and Frank Kunz, East Fourth street and a host of nieces and nephews.

The remains were removed from her home on East Cleveland street to the Jauman funeral home on North Franklin street, where the remains will be in state until the time of funeral services.

Last rites will take place Monday morning at 9:30 o'clock at St. John's Catholic church. Burial will be made in St. John's cemetery.

h. **Frank Kunz** was born on April 5, 1867 in Delphos, Ohio. He was christened on May 30, 1867 in Delphos St. John the Evangelist Catholic Church. He married Catherine M. Shumaker October 25, 1893 in Delphos, Ohio. Frank was a Carpenter and Farmer and resided in Delphos, Ohio. He died on November 7, 1949 in Delphos, Ohio. He was buried on November 10, 1949 in Delphos St. John's Cemetery, Section B, Lot 12, Grave 8. Cause of Death: Heart Attack.

Obituary Delphos Herald November 1949:
FRANK KUNZ DIES MONDAY
Frank Kunz, 641 East Fourth Street, died at 7:50 a.m. Monday at his home after an illness of three months. Death was due to a heart attack. He was born April 5, 1867 southeast of Delphos, the son of Frank and Margaret Kunz. At the time of his death he was 82 years, 7 months, and 2 days of age.

In 1893, he was married in Delphos to Miss Catherine Schumaker, who died June 2, 1931. Surviving are a daughter, Mrs. Forest Gudakunst, at home and a son, Albert Kunz, Detroit and 7 grandchildren. He was a retired farmer and carpenter.

Funeral services will be held at the Oscar A. Kolkmeyer funeral home with the Rev. E. E. Stopher in charge at 10:00 a.m. Thursday. Burial will be in St. John's cemetery.

Pallbearers were the following: Wm. Roth, Oscar Shellabarger, Edward Lause, Lewis Leonard, Frank Grothouse and Henry Wannemacher.

10. **Josiah Clawson, Jr.** was born on March 8, 1844 in Delphos, Ohio to Josiah Clawson, Sr. and Elizabeth Hire. He married Malinda Emily Hartshorn March 22, 1866 in Allen County, Ohio. He was a Farmer and resided in Delphos, Ohio. He served in the American Civil War 118th O.V.I. in Tennessee. He died on March 19, 1922 in Delphos, Ohio. He was buried on March 23, 1922 in Delphos Walnut Grove Cemetery.

Obituary Delphos Herald March 20, 1922:

AGED VETERAN PASSES AWAY

Josiah Clawson Answers Final Summons of Death Sunday Afternoon at Home on Douglas Street – Was Civil War Veteran – Funeral Thursday Afternoon at M.E. Church.

Josiah Clawson, one of Delphos' oldest and most respected citizens, passed away Sunday afternoon at 3:10 o'clock at the family home, 232 North Douglas Street. Mr. Clawson was ailing for several weeks, but was confined to his bed but about three days previous to his death. Infirmities due to his advanced age caused his demise.

Mr. Clawson was born in Allen County, son of Mr. and Mrs. Josiah Clawson, Sr., on March 8, 1844. He was a few days over seventy-eight years of age at the time of his death and spent practically his entire life in Allen County. His birthplace was the homestead near the Hartshorn Cemetery and he spent his early life there. The deceased was a veteran of the Civil War and served four years after which he was honorably discharged.

His marriage to Miss Malinda Hartshorn took place in March 1866. Mr. and Mrs. Clawson were married fifty-four years when Mrs. Clawson was called by death. She passed away three years ago last December 23.

Mr. Clawson's occupation during most of his life was farming. Eight years ago, he retired and the family moved to this city to reside.

Twelve children were born to Mr. and Mrs. Clawson, five of whom are now deceased. Mr. Clawson is survived by seven children, one sister, three half-brothers, ten grandchildren and six great-grandchildren.

He was a member of the Methodist church, of the I.O.O.F., and the Rebekah lodges, and the G.A.R.

The funeral will be held Thursday afternoon at two o'clock at the Methodist church, Rev. Deaton officiating. Interment will follow in Walnut Grove Cemetery.

Delphos Herald March 24, 1922:
LAST RITES: LAST SAD RITES FOR J. CLAWSON HELD THURSDAY – CIVIL WAR VETERAN INTERRED WITH MILITARY HONORS – I.O.O.F. AND REBEKAHS ATTEND SERVICES – HONORARY PALLBEARERS ARE G.A.R. MEMBERS.

Services were held Thursday Afternoon at two o'clock at the Methodist church over the remains of Josiah Clawson, Rev. W. A. Deaton officiating. The last rites were very largely attended, as Mr. Clawson was well known in this vicinity.

Special music during the services was furnished by Mrs. Ed Lybarger and Mrs. J. Wolfe, with Mrs. Clarence Judkins, organist. A beautiful solo was rendered by Mrs. Rose Fast.

The Odd Fellows and the Rebekahs, Mr. Clawson having been a member of both lodges, attended the services in a body and the former had charge at the church and also at the grave in Walnut Grove cemetery.

Honorary pallbearers were selected from among the G.A.R. They were Isaac Ludwig, J. N. Cochran, Jasper Brotherton, Mr. Eggeman, of Ft. Jennings, and Evan H. Jones. The casket and hearse were draped in large American flags, as Mr. Clawson was a veteran of the Civil War.

Acting pallbearers were John Friend, John Wade, Forg Irick, T. N. Bellis, Will Steinle and Joseph Weisgerber.

11. **Malinda Emily Hartshorn** was born on November 2, 1850 in Delphos, Ohio to Elmore Hartshorn and Casander McHenry. She married Josiah Clawson on March 22, 1866 in Allen County, Ohio. She died on December 23, 1918 in Delphos, Ohio. She was buried on December 26, 1918 in Delphos Walnut Grove Cemetery.

Obituary Delphos Herald December 23, 1918:
MRS. CLAWSON DIED MONDAY AT 9 O'CLOCK
WIFE OF JOSIAH CLAWSON PASSED AWAY AFTER ILLNESS
OF SIX MONTHS DURATION – WAS LIFE-LONG RESIDENT
OF THIS VICINITY – FUNERAL AT METHODIST CHURCH
THURSDAY AFTERNOON AT TWO O'CLOCK.

After an illness of six months of a complication of diseases, Mrs. Malinda Emily Clawson, wife of Josiah Clawson, died at nine o'clock, Monday morning. Mrs. Clawson's death occurred at the family home on the corner of Douglas and Third streets, and was not unexpected, as she had been in very serious condition for some time.

The deceased was a life-long resident of this vicinity, having been born on a farm near the Auglaize river, in Allen county, on November 2, 1850. She was the daughter of Mr. and Mrs. Elmer Hartshorn.

She grew to womanhood on the farm and was married to Mr. Clawson there on March 22, 1866. Mr. and Mrs. Clawson made their home east of town until five years ago, when they moved to this city.

Twelve children were born to Mr. and Mrs. Clawson, three of whom died in infancy and one son, Roy, having passed away exactly seven weeks previous to his mother's death.

Mrs. Clawson leaves to mourn her departure, her husband, and the following children: Mrs. John Allen, of Gates Mills, Ohio, Mrs. Fred Kunz, and Mrs. Glen Fosnaugh, of near Delphos; Mrs. George Bly and Mrs. Joseph Louth, of Van Wert; Harry, Fanny and Van, at home. A sister Mrs. A. J. Eckfeld, of Marion, one half-sister, Mrs. Bertha Conner, of New Baltimore, and one half-brother, Clarence Hartshorn, of Toledo, also survive.

She was a very active member of the Methodist church previous to her failing health and will be greatly missed by her associates in church work. She was a member of the Home and Foreign Missionary Society of the Methodist church and also of the Rebecca lodge of this city.

The funeral will be held Thursday afternoon at two o'clock at the Methodist church, Rev. Bussard officiating. Interment will be made in Walnut Grove cemetery.

Josiah Clawson and Malinda Emily Hartshorn had the following children:

a.   **Nellie E. Clawson** was born in 1867. She married John W. Allen in 1887. She died in 1947. She was buried in Delphos Walnut Grove Cemetery.

b.   **Fannie May Clawson** was born on March 20, 1870 in Delphos, Ohio. She died on August 25, 1952 in Lima, Ohio. She was buried in Delphos Walnut Grove Cemetery. Fannie never married. Her son, Van Lyndell Clawson, was raised by her parents, Josiah and Malinda Clawson.

c.   **Deflora Alice "Flo" Clawson (# 5 on chart)** was born on May 25, 1873. She was married to Frederick Kunz.

d.   **Iona Ethel "Bessie" Clawson** was born on November 2, 1879 in Van Wert County, Ohio. She married John Kruger, George Bly and Edward Mullenhour. She died in 1958 in Lima, Ohio. She was buried in Delphos Walnut Grove Cemetery.

e.   **Virgil Josiah Clawson** was born in 1880. He died in 1880.

f.   **Harry Lewis Clawson** was born on February 14, 1882 in Putnam County, Ohio. He married Theresia M. Niemeyer in 1904 and Amanda S. Hunt on October 3, 1936. He resided in Delphos, Ohio. He was retired from the State Highway Department. He was a Methodist. He died on July 31, 1967 in Delphos, Ohio. He was buried on August 2, 1967 in Delphos Walnut Grove Cemetery.

g.   **Monna Frances Clawson** was born on January 11, 1887 in Allen County, Ohio. She married Glen Fosnaugh August 11, 1906. She died in Lacombe, Alberta, Canada. She was buried in Lacombe Fairview Cemetery.

h.   **Roy Edward Clawson** was born on September 20, 1889 in Delphos, Ohio. He was a R.R. Laborer. He was a Methodist. He died on November 11, 1918 in Delphos, Ohio. He was buried in Delphos Walnut Grove Cemetery. Cause of Death: Influenza epidemic of 1918.

> i. **Cleo Katherine Clawson** was born in 1897. She married Joseph Louth. She died on November 9, 1980 in Lima, Ohio. She was buried in Woodlawn Cemetery, Lima, Ohio.

12. **Frederick J. Lause** was born on March 2, 1825 in Melle, Hanover, Germany to Henry Joseph Lause and Mary Elizabeth Giesker. Frederick came to America in 1844 with his parents. He was married to Mary A. Pohlman on April 3, 1856 in Delphos, Ohio. He was a Farmer. He died on March 19, 1897 in Delphos, Ohio. He was buried on March 22, 1897 in Delphos St. John's OLD Cemetery, Section A, Row 4, Grave 61A.

History of Allen County, Ohio 1885
Warner, Beers and Company (pages 644-645)
    FREDERICK LAUSE, farmer, P.O. Delphos, was born in Hanover, Germany, March 2, 1825, son of Henry and Mary (Giesker) Lause, who were parents of seven children: Henry, Catharine, Elisabeth (deceased), Mary, Frederick, Elisabeth and Clara. Our subject received a common school education, and learned the carpenter's trade in his native land, coming to America when twenty years of age, and locating in this county. He purchased his present farm in 1850, and from a forest has transformed it into one of the best farms of Marion Township. His fine residence was erected during the summer of 1884. Mr. Lause was married April 3, 1856 to Mary Pohlman, born in Hanover, Germany, May 2, 1838, and who was brought to America when six years old. Her parents, Casper and Clara (Henseler) Pohlmann, had the following children: John, Mary and Clemens (living); Elisabeth, Henry, Joseph, Theresia, Anna, Catharina and Clara (deceased.) Twelve children were born to our subject and wife: Mary, Elisabeth (deceased), Dina, Casper, Henry (deceased), Frank, Clara, Anna, Clemens, Joseph, Frederick and Aloysius. The family are consistent members of the Catholic Church.

History of Allen County, Ohio and Representative Citizens 1906
Edited And Compiled By Charles C. Miller, Ph D.
    FREDERICK LAUSE was born to Henry and Mary (Giesker) Lause in Hanover Germany on March 2, 1825. Here he attended the common schools and then learned the carpenter's trade with Mr.

Pohlman. In 1844 he came to America, locating in Allen County, where in 1850 he purchased a farm in Marion township. The country was all forest at that time and to settlers less robust and courageous than was Mr. Lause, the clearing and cultivating of this land, within the limits of a lifetime, would have seemed an impossible task. But he had come to America to found a home and in the years that followed no discouragement of hardship was too great to interrupt his industry or dampen his enthusiasm. He lived to see the forest cleared and the land developed into a rich agricultural estate. The old homestead in section 31 is still occupied by his widow and a son, A. W. Lause.

Frederick Lause was married on April 3, 1856, to Mary Pohlman, who was born in Hanover, Germany, May 2, 1838. When six years of age she accompanied her parents to America. They were Casper and Clara (Henseler) Pohlman. Casper Pohlman was one of the original colony to settle in Section 10 as Delphos was first called, and he crossed the Atlantic on the same sailing vessel which brought here the late venerable Rev. John Otto Bredeick, the founder of Delphos and the organizer of the Catholic Church at Delphos, known as the Church of St. John the Evangelist.

Casper Pohlman was a carpenter and his work, with that of his son-in-law, Frederick Lause, may still be seen in Marion township. This locality soon outgrew log houses, and for many years the two men worked almost constantly in season, at their trade. Mr. and Mrs. Pohlman had 10 children, the two survivors being: Mary, the wife of Frederick Lause, and Clemens, who resides in section 19, Marion township.

In the summer of 1884, Frederick Lause erected on his farm above mentioned, a fine farm residence, one of the commodious and comfortable homes of the locality. Here his last years were passed and here his wife and son enjoy comforts provided by his years of industry. The following children were born to Frederick Lause and wife, namely: Mary, wife of John Lauer, of Ottawa, Ohio; Dinah, wife of John Laudick, a farmer living in Kansas; Casper, of Marion township; Henry, deceased; Frank, a farmer of Marion Township; Clara, wife of A. J. Smith, of Topeka, Kansas; Anna, deceased; Clemens, a farmer of Marion Township; Joseph, a blacksmith in the village of Landeck; Frederick, of Marion Township; and Aloysius W., of Marion Township.

All this family are consistent members of the Church of St. John the Evangelist.

13. **Mary A. Pohlman** was born on May 2, 1838 in Melle, Hanover, Germany to Casper H. Pohlman and Clara Maria Henseler. Mary came to America in 1844 with her parents. She was married to Frederick J. Lause on April 3, 1956 in Delphos, Ohio. She was Catholic. She died on August 22, 1910 in Delphos, Ohio. She was buried on August 26, 1910 in Delphos St. John's OLD Cemetery, Section A, Row 4, Grave 61B.

Obituary Delphos Herald August 23, 1910:
AGED LADY IS DEAD
MRS. MARY LAUSE PASSED AWAY MONDAY NIGHT
Came to Delphos When This Section Was Vast Wilderness.
Came to America on Ship That Carried Father Bredeick.

One of Marion township's old and well known citizens passed away Monday night, in the person of Mrs. Mary Lause. Mrs. Lause had been in failing health for some time, the infirmities of old age having a telling effect upon her. For the past ten months she had been in a practically helpless condition from paralysis and a complication of diseases. During the week preceding her death she had grown much weaker, but it was not thought that her death would come soon and her demise was somewhat unexpected to the family. She had been sitting up Monday evening, but at about 10:45 suffered a fainting spell and passed away in a few minutes, the family scarcely realizing that the end had come. Her death occurred at the home of her son, A. W. Lause, south of Delphos.

Mary Ann Pohlman was born in Melle, Hanover, Germany, May 2, 1838, and died August 22, 1910, at the age of 72 years, 3 months and 20 days. She came to America in 1844, at the age of six years, on the same ship that brought Fr. Bredeick to this country. She came to Delphos with her parents when this section was one vast unbroken wilderness and has lived here ever since. She was among those sturdy pioneers who underwent hardships and assisted in transforming the then wild country to its present expanse of productive fields instead of forests and swamps. On April 3, 1856, she was united in marriage to Frederick J. Lause, in Delphos, the ceremony being performed by Rev. Fr. Bredeick. To this union were born twelve children, seven sons and five daughters. Two sons and two daughters preceded their mother in death, one son, Joseph Lause, having died four weeks ago. The surviving children are: Mrs. John Lauer of Ottoville, Mrs. John Laudick of Windhorst, Kansas, Mrs. G. A. Schmidt of Topeka, Kansas, Casper Lause of south of Delphos, Frank Lause and Clemens Lause of near Landeck, Fred Lause of south of Delphos and A. W. Lause of South of Delphos. She also leaves 37 grandchildren and 10 great-grandchildren. Mr. Lause preceded her in death thirteen years ago last March. Clem Pohlman of east of Delphos is a brother of the deceased.

Mrs. Lause was of a retiring disposition, was kind and always had the welfare of her family a heart and in her death the community has lost a good citizen and the family a devoted mother. The family will have the sympathy of all in their sad bereavement.

Mrs. Lause was a devoted member of St. John's Catholic church and was also a member of the Sacred Heart League and the Altar Society of that church. The funeral will be held from the church Friday morning at 9 o'clock and interment will be made in St. John's Cemetery.

Frederick J. Lause and Mary A. Pohlman had the following children:

   a. **Mary Elizabeth Lause** was born on January 26, 1857 in Delphos, Ohio. She married John Lauer May 12, 1881. She resided in Ottawa, Ohio.

   b. **Clara Maria Lause** was born on November 4, 1858 in Delphos, Ohio. She died on May 4, 1866. She was buried on May 7, 1866 in Delphos St. John's Cemetery.

   c. **Bernardina Mary Lause** was born on February 1, 1861 in Delphos, Ohio. She married John C. Laudick September 9, 1886 at Delphos, Ohio. She resided in Kansas. She died on November 9, 1946 in Spearville, Kansas.

   d. **Casper J. Lause** was born on December 6, 1862 in Allen County, Ohio. He married Elizabeth Trentman June 17, 1886 at Delphos, Ohio. He was a Farmer. He died on June 6, 1942 in Columbus, Ohio. He was buried on June 8, 1942 in Delphos St. John's Cemetery.

e. **John Henry Lause** was born on October 17, 1864 in Delphos, Ohio. He died on January 26, 1867 at Delphos, Ohio. He was buried on January 28, 1867 in Delphos St. John's Cemetery.

f. **Frank J. Lause** was born on January 9, 1867 in Allen County, Ohio. He married Elizabeth Neimeyer November 16, 1893. He died on May 6, 1924 in Putnam County, Ohio. He was buried on May 10, 1924 in Delphos St. John's Cemetery. Cause of Death: Drowned in the Auglaize River.

g. **Clara Elizabeth Lause** was born on October 1, 1868 in Delphos, Ohio. She married A. J. Smith and Charles Moore. She resided in Kansas and Everett, Washington.

h. **Anna Catherine Lause** was born on January 14, 1871 in Delphos, Ohio. She married Joseph Kroeger September 14, 1898. She died on March 20, 1900. She was buried on March 23, 1900 in Delphos St. John's Cemetery.

i. **Clemens Frederick Lause** was born on September 23, 1872 in Delphos, Ohio. He married Anna Barbara Bonifas September 4, 1900 at Landeck, Ohio. He resided in Delphos, Ohio. He was a Laborer at the Cigar Factory. He died on November 23, 1956 in Lima, Ohio. He was buried on November 26, 1956 in Delphos St. John's Cemetery.

j. **Joseph Frederick Lause** was born on September 5, 1874 in Delphos, Ohio. He married Mary Kroeger September 7, 1897. He was a Blacksmith in Landeck, Ohio. He died on July 24, 1910. He was buried on July 27, 1910 in Delphos St. John's Cemetery.

k. **Frederick J. Lause II (# 6 on chart)** was born on December 29, 1875. He married Helena Maria "Lena" Moreo.

l. **Aloysius William Lause** was born on January 24, 1880 in Delphos, Ohio. He married Anna Gerdeman June 9, 1903. He resided in Delphos, Ohio. He died on July 26, 1962 in

Delphos, Ohio. He was buried on July 30, 1962 in Delphos St. John's Cemetery.

14. **Andrew Moreo** was born on June 5, 1844 in Bavaria, Germany to J. Philippi Morio and Margaret Seibel. He was married to Catharina Lang November 23, 1869 in Hauenstein, Pfalz, Bayern. He married Christina Caroline Loy on August 23, 1877 at Landeck, Ohio. He was a Farmer. He was a Catholic. He died on March 16, 1937 in Delphos, Ohio. He was buried on March 19, 1937 in Delphos St. John's Cemetery, Section O, Lot 21, Grave 1.

Andrew Moreo had 5 children with his first wife, Catherine. After Catherine died, he remarried to Christina Loy and they had 6 children. Andrew and Christina (Loy) Moreo lived on a farm in Marion township, Allen County, Ohio near Landeck. (East about ½ mile, then north in a lane between two houses.) The 1880 plat book shows 40 acres under name of Monroe. In 1977 no house existed on the 40 acres but the neighbors knew it as the Moreo place. Andrew and Christina moved to 609 S. Clay Street in Delphos, Ohio before World War I.

15. **Christina Caroline Loy** was born on September 25, 1857 in Van Wert County, Ohio to John Loy I and Susanna Schneider. She was christened on April 5, 1874 in Delphos St. John's Catholic Church by Rev. Hoeffel. Her sponsors were Michael Sommers and Martha Dolt. She married Andrew Moreo on August 23, 1877 at Landeck, Ohio. She died on October 23, 1936 in Delphos, Ohio. She was buried on October 26, 1936 in Delphos St. John's Cemetery, Section O, Lot 21, Grave 2.

Andrew Moreo and Christina Caroline Loy had the following children:

a. **Marguerite Sarah Moreo** was born on September 30, 1878 in Landeck, Ohio. She was christened on October 1, 1878 in Landeck St. John Church. She married John Martin Murray on May 19, 1897 at Delphos, Ohio. She resided in Delphos, Ohio. She died on December 28, 1944 in Lima, Ohio. She was buried on January 2, 1945 in Delphos St. John's Cemetery.

b. **Mary E. Moreo** was born on December 22, 1880 in Landeck, Ohio. She was christened on December 23, 1880 in Landeck St. John Church. She married Frank A. Vogt on May 8, 1900 at Greenville, Wood County, Ohio. She married Clement A. Kohorst on October 20, 1921 at Delphos, Ohio. She resided in Delphos, Ohio. She died on July 28, 1967 in Cridersville, Ohio. She was buried on July 31, 1967 in Delphos St. John's Cemetery.

c. **Helena Maria "Lena" Moreo (# 7 on chart)** was born on September 13, 1882. She married Frederick J. Lause II.

d. **John A. Moreo** was born on April 29, 1886 in Landeck, Ohio. He married Louise Simmons on October 7, 1913. He resided in Perrysburg, Ohio. He died on July 21, 1970 in Maumee, Ohio. He was buried in Perrysburg St. Rose Cemetery.

e. **Susan C. Moreo** was born on July 6, 1889 in Landeck, Ohio. She married Charles Lucius on May 10, 1910. She resided in Delphos, Ohio. She died on January 30, 1973 in Lima, Ohio. She was buried on February 2, 1973 in Landeck St. John the Baptist Cemetery.

f. **Lawrence C. Moreo** was born on October 20, 1892 in Landeck, Ohio. He married Helen Wolf. He resided in Delphos, Ohio. He died on December 31, 1957 in Lima, Ohio. He was buried on January 3, 1958 in Delphos St. John's Cemetery.

FIFTH GENERATION

16. **Franz Anton Kunz** was born about 1786 in Bavaria to Jacob Kunz and Margaretha Franzoni. He was married to Margaretha Feinholz. He resided in Rheinzabern, Bavaria, Germany. He was a Farmer. He died on February 11, 1844 in Rheinzabern, Bavaria.
Source: Register office of Rheinzabern
From Birth entry and Marriage entry of son, Franz Michael Kunz.

17. **Margaretha Feinholz** was born in Bavaria. She married Franz Anton Kunz. She resided in Rheinzabern, Bavaria, Germany. She died on December 15, 1836 in Rheinzabern, Bavaria.
Source: Register office of Rheinzabern
From Birth entry and Marriage entry of son, Franz Michael Kunz.

Franz Anton Kunz and Margaretha Feinholz had the following children:

      a.   **Franz Michael Kunz (# 8 on chart)** was born on May 22, 1819. He was married to Margaretha Marz.

18. **Franz Michael Marz** was born about 1768 or 1778 in Bavaria. He married Maria Anna Himmelsbach. He resided in Rheinzabern, Bavaria. He was a farmer.
Source: Register Office of Rheinzabern
From Birth entry and Marriage entry of daughter, Margaretha Marz.

According to the Marriage entry of his daughter, Margaretha Marz, he was 79 years of age in 1847. If he was 41 years of age when Margaretha was born, he would have been 69 years old in 1847. Franz Michael Marz was either born about 1768 or 1778.

19. **Maria Anna Himmelsbach** was born in Bavaria. She married Franz Michael Marz. She died on December 4, 1829 in Rheinzabern, Bavaria.
Source: Register Office of Rheinzabern
From Birth entry and Marriage entry of daughter, Margaretha Marz.

Franz Michael Marz and Maria Anna Himmelsbach had the following children:

    a. **Margaretha Marz (# 9 on chart)** was born on April 3, 1819. She was married to Franz Michael Kunz.

20. **Josiah Clawson, Sr.** was born about 1799 in Columbia, Hamilton Co., Ohio to Mr. and Mrs. Thomas Clawson. He was married to Martha Russell on March 1, 1823 at Shelby County, Ohio. He was married to Elizabeth Hire on December 19, 1833 in Allen County, Ohio. He was a Farmer and Storekeeper. His religion was Baptist. He resided in Allen County near Fort Amanda about 1828. He died on February 6, 1844 in Allen County, Ohio. He was buried in Hartshorn Cemetery Delphos, Ohio.

21. **Elizabeth Hire** was born on July 14, 1817 in Fayette County, Ohio to Martin Hire and Sarah or Sally Neely. She was married to Josiah Clawson , Sr. on December 19, 1833 in Allen County, Ohio. She was married to David Whirrett on May 14, 1848. She died on August 2, 1889 in Allen County, Ohio. She was buried in Hartshorn Cemetery, Delphos, Ohio.

History Book:
Mrs. Elizabeth Whirrett was born July 14, 1817, in Fayette County, Ohio and came to Allen County with her father, Martin Hire, in 1824. In December, 1835, she was married to Josiah Clawson. Five children were born to them: Lauretta, who died at five years of age; William, who lived to the age of forty-two years; Martha, who is the wife of Augustus Tabner, of Van Wert; Sarah, wife of Wesley Allen, of Putnam County; and Josiah, now living in Putnam County. Mr. Clawson died February 6, 1844. Four years afterwards Mrs. Clawson married David Whirrett. By this union four children were born, all of whom are now living: Benjamin Franklin, living in Marion township, whose wife was Miss Maggie Fair; Thomas Jefferson, who married Miss Hannah Otem, and now lives in Putnam County; Jacob Neely, living at home; and John Fremont, who married Miss Elizabeth Kramer, and lives in Marion township. Mrs. Whirrett is the mother of nine children, and has twenty-two grandchildren. Is sixty-five years of age, and enjoys health and strength. Coming to this country at an

early day, she had to endure the hardships incidental to pioneer life, but is well preserved for a woman of her age, and possesses all her faculties to a good degree. She remembers many of the settlers of that time, and can relate numerous interesting incidents of backwoods life. Mr. Whirrett died April 5, 1870.

Josiah Clawson, Sr. and Elizabeth Hire had the following children:

    a. **Lauretta Clawson** was born after 1834. She died about 1839 at 5 years old.

    b. **William Clawson** was born in 1837 in Allen County, Ohio. He married Asby Jenkins August 1, 1861 at Allen County, Ohio. He died on October 10, 1879 in Allen County, Ohio. He was buried in Delphos Walnut Grove Cemetery.

    c. **Martha L. Clawson** was born in 1839. She married August Luebner November 17, 1861 in Allen County, Ohio. She resided in Van Wert, Ohio.

    d. **Sarah Clawson** was born in 1842. She married Wesley Allen May 12, 1864 in Allen County, Ohio. She died in 1918. She was buried in Delphos Walnut Grove Cemetery.

    e. **Josiah Clawson, Jr. (# 10 on chart)** was born on March 8, 1844. He was married to Malinda Emily Hartshorn.

22. **Elmore Hartshorn** was born in 1815 in Ohio to Edward Hartshorn, Sr. and Lydia DeLong. He was married to Casander McHenry September 29, 1836 in Putnam County, Ohio. He was a Lawyer at Delphos, Ohio. He was married to Anna E. Cowen in 1860. He died on January 26, 1877. He was buried in Hartshorn Cemetery, Delphos, Ohio.

Delphos Weekly Herald Thursday Feb 1, 1877:
DEATH OF A PIONEER

Elmore Hartshorn a well known citizen and Lawyer of this city died on Friday morning January 26, age 61 years. The deceased was one of the early pioneers of this vicinity where he resided continuously for a period of 46 years. He was a man of generous impulses and gentlemanly instincts whose position in life might have been one of prominence if not of eminence but for a frailty which is human but destructive. The funeral ceremonies took place on Sunday morning at Methodist Church and were very largely attended. He leaves a widow and number of children who have the sympathy of the community.

23. **Casander McHenry** was born in 1816 in Ohio to Isaac McHenry and Jemima Gaskill. She married Elmore Hartshorn September 29, 1836 in Putnam County, Ohio. She died on December 20, 1859. She was buried in Hartshorn Cemetery, Delphos, Ohio.

Elmore Hartshorn and Casander McHenry had the following children:

   a.   **Mary Ann Hartshorn** was born in 1841. She was married to Mardica Pangle on March 28, 1861 in Allen County, Ohio.

   b.   **George Edward Hartshorn** was born in 1845 in Marion Twp, Allen County, Ohio. He was married to Kate Cook and Ellen Thompson. He died on March 22, 1911 in Marion Twp, Allen County, Ohio. He was buried on March 24, 1911 in Walnut Grove Cemetery in Delphos, Ohio.

   Obituary Delphos Herald March 22, 1911:
   George Hartshorn Summoned from Time to Eternity.
   George Hartshorn, a veteran of the Civil war, and a well-known stationery engineer, died at 5 o'clock Wednesday morning at the home of his sister, Mrs. Josiah Clawson, about three and a half miles east of Delphos, the culmination of a brief illness due to cancer which attacked Mr. Hartshorn's cheek.
   Deceased was about 67 years old and was born in Marion Township. During the Civil war he was a member of Company F, 118th O.V.I., Captain Ruel's company, and served three years. At the time of his death Mr. Hartshorn was the Commander of Ruel Post G.A.R., of Delphos. Mr. Hartshorn had lived in Delphos a number of years. He was

twice married, his wives preceding him in death. He has four children.

Mrs. Josiah Clawson, at whose home he died, and Mrs. Eckfeld of Marion, Ohio, formerly of Delphos, are sisters of the deceased. Mrs. Eckfeld is a nurse and was with her brother in his last illness.

Funeral services will be held over the remains at Morris Chapel church Friday afternoon and interment will be made in Walnut Grove cemetery. The cortege will leave the Clawson home at 1 p.m., and the funeral will be conducted by Rev. G. B. Wiltsie, pastor of the Delphos M.E. church.

c. **Lydia Hartshorn** was born in January 1848. She died on February 28, 1850. She was buried in Hartshorn Cemetery, Delphos, Ohio.

d. **Malinda Emily Hartshorn (# 11 on chart)** was born on November 2, 1850. She was married to Josiah Clawson.

e. **Frances Louise Hartshorn** was born in 1854. She resided in Marion, Ohio before 1911. She was a Nurse. She was married to Abraham Eckfeld.

24. **Henry Joseph Lause** was born on August 4, 1791 in Wellingholzhausen, Hanover, Germany to Johann Heinrich Grothaus and Catharina Gertrude Lause. He was married to Mary Elizabeth Giesker in Germany. Henry came to America in 1844 with wife and 5 children on the ship ISABELLA. They arrived in New York on Sept. 20, 1844 and settled in Delphos Ohio. He was a Farmer. He died before 1847 in Delphos, Ohio. He was buried in Delphos St. John's Cemetery.
AKA: Joseph Henry Lause.

25. **Mary Elizabeth Giesker** was born between 1788 and 1793 in Melle, Hanover, Germany. She was married to Henry Joseph Lause in Germany. She died on February 10, 1860 in Delphos, Ohio. She was buried on February 11, 1860 in Delphos St. John's Cemetery.

Henry Joseph Lause and Mary Elizabeth Giesker had the following children:

   a. **Balthasar Henerious Lause** was born on March 20, 1819 or 1820 in Melle, Hanover, Germany. He came to America in 1844 with his parents. He married Elizabeth Mary Miller on April 10, 1849 in Delphos, Ohio. He died on November 15, 1871 in Delphos, Ohio. He was buried on November 18, 1871 in Delphos St. John's Cemetery.

   b. **Clara Maria Lause** was born on September 21, 1820 in Melle, Hanover, Germany. She came to America in 1844 with her parents. She married J. Casper Mesker on April 28, 1845 in Delphos, Ohio. She died on June 26, 1919 in Delphos, Ohio. She was buried on June 30, 1919 in Delphos St. John's Cemetery.

   c. **Catherine Lause** was born in 1822 in Melle, Hanover, Germany. Catherine was not on the Ship to America with her family.

   d. **Elizabeth Lause** was born in 1823 in Melle, Hanover, Germany. She died in Germany as a young child. She was buried in Germany.

   e. **Frederick J. Lause (# 12 on chart)** was born on March 2, 1825. He was married to Mary A. Pohlman.

   f. **Mary Lause** was born in 1830 in Melle, Hanover, Germany. She came to America in 1844 with her parents. She was married to Andrew Glucky. She resided in Dayton, Ohio.

   g. **Elizabeth Maria Lause** was born in 1830 in Melle, Hanover, Germany. She came to America in 1844 with her parents. She was married to Joseph W. Schwartzengraber. She died on April 15, 1906. She was buried on April 18, 1906 in Delphos St. John's Cemetery, Section G, Lot 1, Grave 2. (75y 11m 15d)

26. **Casper H. Pohlman** was born about 1803 in Wellingholzhausen, Hanover, Germany. He was married to Clara Maria Henseler in

Germany. He was a Farmer. He died on June 27, 1880. He was buried on June 29, 1880 in Delphos St. John's Cemetery.

Casper, his wife, Clara, and children came to America in October of 1844 on the Ship Isabella with Rev. John Otto Bredeick. They arrived in New York. They settled on a farm east of Delphos in what is now Marion Township, Allen County, Ohio. After coming to Delphos, Casper worked at his trade, building churches, mills, etc., in different parts of the country. The 1865 census refers to him as a farmer. Casper died in June of 1880. He was between 76 and 81 years of age at the time of his death. He is buried at St. John's Catholic Cemetery in Delphos, Ohio.

27. **Clara Maria Henseler** was born about 1810 in Melle, Hanover, Germany. She was married to Casper H. Pohlman in Germany. She died on August 23, 1876 in Delphos, Ohio. She was buried on August 24, 1876 in Delphos St. John's Cemetery. She was Catholic.

Casper H. Pohlman and Clara Maria Henseler had the following children:

   a.   **Catharina Pohlman** died before 1911.

   b.   **Clara Pohlman** died before 1911.

   c.   **John H. Pohlman** was born on August 15, 1833. He was a Farmer. He died on April 17, 1895. He was buried on April 19, 1895 in Delphos St. John's Cemetery.

   d.   **Henry Pohlman** was born about 1834. He died before 1911.

   e.   **Anna Maria Pohlman** was born about 1838. She died before 1911.

   f.   **Mary A. Pohlman (# 13 on chart)** was born on May 2, 1838. She was married to Frederick J. Lause.

   g.   **Clemens Pohlman** was born on October 2, 1840 in Melle, Hanover, Germany. He was married to Bernadina Brinkman June 21, 1865 in Delphos, Ohio. He died on March 21, 1911 in Delphos, Ohio. He was buried on March 25, 1911 in Delphos St. John's Cemetery.

Obituary Delphos Herald March 22, 1911:
Clemens Pohlman Summoned from Time to Eternity.

Clemens Pohlman died at 2:40 o'clock Tuesday afternoon at the family home about half a mile east of Delphos, after a lingering illness from paralysis, attended by the infirmities of old age.

Deceased was born in Hanover, Germany, in the neighborhood of the town of Melle, October 2, 1840. In October of 1844, his parents, Casper and Clara Pohlman, the father a carpenter and wood worker, came to America and located on the farm just east of Delphos where the subject of this sketch died.

At the time there were only a few families in this territory and Delphos was known as Section 10. The canal had been opened in the spring of the same year that the family located here. Casper Pohlman died in 1881 at the age of 81 years, and his wife passed away in 1876 in her sixty-sixth year. Rev. Father John Otto Bredeick, the founder of Delphos and St. John's Catholic congregation, came to America on the same ship with Mr. Pohlman.

Clemens Pohlman was only four years old when his parents came to Delphos. He had ten brothers and sister, all of whom preceded him in death. He was educated in St. Mary's college in Cleveland and in 1865 was united in marriage to Bernadina Brinkman, who was born in Glandorf, Putnam county. Seven children were born to this union, three of whom have passed away. Surviving are John Pohlman and Mrs. John Jauman, living at the home place. Mrs. Joseph Weisgerber of Delphos, and Mrs. Charles Stanton of Akron.

Mr. Pohlman assisted in converting this part of the country from a wilderness into one of the most fertile garden spots of the earth, and during the sixty-six years of his life as a resident of Allen county saw the forests give way to broad fields of waving grain, the swamps replaced by fertile lands, and peace and plenty take the place of pioneer hardships. Mr. Pohlman's father engaged in the building of churches, mills etc., all over this section. The elder Mr. Pohlman added to his acreage until they numbered seventy, and to his son, by frugality and toil and honest dealings as an agriculturist, added still more and he leaves to his children a farm of 100 acres.

Mr. Pohlman was of a quiet and retiring disposition, a splendid citizen and neighbor and the cry of the distressed and needy in his ears always found response in the way of assistance. He was 70 years old last October.

Deceased was a faithful member of St. John's church, a member of St. Joseph's society and the Sacred Heart League. The funeral services will take place at St. John's church at 9:30 o'clock Saturday morning and interment will be made in the East Side cemetery.

h. **Mary Elizabeth Pohlman** was born about 1843. She died on January 28, 1864. She was buried on January 30, 1864 in Delphos St. John's Cemetery.

i. **John Pohlman** was born on March 7, 1846 in Delphos, Ohio. He died on June 7, 1847. He was buried on June 9, 1847.

j. **Theresia Pohlman** was born on April 25, 1848 in Delphos, Ohio. She died before 1911.

k. **Joseph Pohlman** was born on August 6, 1851 in Delphos, Ohio. He died on August 14, 1872.

28. **J. Philippi Morio** was born in 1806 in Bavaria, Germany to Johannes Andreas Morio and Anna Maria Leibrecht. He was christened in 1806 in Hauenstein, Pfalz, Bayern. He was married to Margaret Seibel on November 15, 1831 in Hauenstein, Pfalz, Bayern. He immigrated to America in 1846. He died on August 13, 1847 in Frenchtown, Seneca County, Ohio. He was buried in New Riegel, Ohio, St. Boniface Cemetery. He was Catholic.

29. **Margaret Seibel** was born in 1810 in Bavaria, Germany to Martini Seibel and Elisabethae Cronauer. She was christened on October 6, 1810 in Hauenstein, Pfalz, Bayern. She married J. Philippi Morio on November 15, 1831 in Hauenstein, Pfalz, Bayern. She died

on February 15, 1882 in Frenchtown, Seneca County, Ohio. She was Catholic.

J. Philippi Morio and Margaret Seibel had the following children:

a. **Lesenzo (Lawrence) Morio** was born in 1833 in Bavaria, Germany.

b. **Barbara Morio** was born in 1840 in Bavaria, Germany She was married to Joseph Eischen on July 7, 1863 in Seneca County, Ohio.

c. **Elizabeth Morio** was born in 1842 in Bavaria, Germany. She was married to Nicolas Siemet on January 21, 1861 in Seneca County, Ohio.

d. **Andrew Moreo (# 14 on chart)** was born on June 5, 1844. He was married to Christina Caroline Loy.

e. **Julia A. Morio** was born in 1846 in Bavaria, Germany. She was married to Matthias Eischen on April 15, 1863 in Seneca County, Ohio.

30. **John Loy I** was born in 1820 in Baden, Germany. He was a Protestant Minister. He was married to Susanna Schneider on March 28, 1857 in Marion County, Ohio. He was married to Mrs. Hydaker before 1846. He was married to Mariah Augustine on December 10, 1863 in Ohio. He died on April 21, 1892 in Delphos, Ohio.

31. **Susanna Schneider** was born in 1834 in Ohio. She was married to John Loy I on March 28, 1857 in Marion County, Ohio.

John Loy I and Susanna Schneider had the following children:

a. **Christina Caroline Loy (# 15 on chart)** was born on September 25, 1857. She was married to Andrew Moreo.

b. **Samuel Loy** was born in 1859 in Ohio. He was married to Margaret Rower.

SIXTH GENERATION

32. Jacob Kunz was married to Margaretha Franzoni. He died on January 15, 1794 in Rheinzabern, Bavaria.
Source: Register office of Rheinzabern - From Marriage entry of grandson, Franz Michael Kunz.

33. Margaretha Franzoni was married to Jacob Kunz. She died on February 17, 1819 in Rheinzabern, Bavaria.
Source: Register office of Rheinzabern - From Marriage entry of grandson, Franz Michael Kunz.

Jacob Kunz and Margaretha Franzoni had the following children:

> a. **Franz Anton Kunz (# 16 on chart)** was born about 1786. He was married to Margaretha Feinholz.

34. Bonifaz Feinholz was married to Elizabeth Reihs. He died on September 15, 1834 in Rheinzabern, Bavaria.
Source: Register office of Rheinzabern - From Marriage entry of grandson, Franz Michael Kunz.

35. Elizabeth Reihs was married to Bonifaz Feinholz. She died on April 18, 1830 in Rheinzabern, Bavaria.
Source: Register office of Rheinzabern - From Marriage entry of grandson, Franz Michael Kunz.

Bonifaz Feinholz and Elizabeth Reihs had the following children:

> a. **Margaretha Feinholz (# 17 on chart)** was born in Bavaria. She was married to Franz Anton Kunz.

36. Thomas Clawson was married to Unknown Wife. He was listed in the 1820 Census of Montgomery County, Ohio, Wayne Township:

Thomas Clawson ...... 45 and over
His wife 26-45
1 son 10-16
3 daughters .... under 10
2 daughters 10-16

37. Mrs. Thomas Clawson was married to Thomas Clawson. Her name is unknown.

Mr. and Mrs. Thomas Clawson had the following children:

> a. **Josiah Clawson, Sr. (# 20 on chart)** was born about 1799. He was married to Elizabeth Hire.

Mr. and Mrs. Thomas Clawson possibly also had the following children:

> b. **Rachel Clawson** was born about 1800 in Pennsylvania or Ohio. She was married to John Patton on January 8, 1823 in Clark County, Ohio. She died on February 15, 1850 in Allen County, Ohio.
>
> c. **Frederick Clawson** was born after 1800. He died in 1844.
>
> d. **Andrew Clawson** was born about 1808 in Ohio. He was married to Mary Kiggins on March 15, 1830 in Shelby County, Ohio.
>
> e. **Mercy Ann Clawson** was born on February 23, 1819 in Ohio. She was married to James Kiggins on November 19, 1837 in Putnam County, Ohio. She died on July 16, 1884 in Allen County, Ohio. She was buried in Delphos Hartshorn Cemetery.

38. Martin Hire was born in 1792 in Hardy or Grant County, West Virginia to Leonard Hire and Catherine Rohrbaugh. He was married to Sally (Sarah) Neely on August 14, 1811 in Ross County, Ohio. He was a Farmer, Carpenter and Cabinet maker. He moved from Fayette County, Ohio to Allen County, Ohio in 1824. He was married to Phebe Bates on November 17, 1847. He died on June 10, 1851 in Auglaize County, Ohio. He was buried in Moulton or Fort Amanda, Ohio.
He was in the Military: War of 1812.

39. Sally (Sarah) Neely married Martin Hire on August 14, 1811 at Ross County, Ohio. She died before 1847. She was buried in Moulton or Fort Amanda, Ohio.

Martin Hire and Sally (Sarah) Neely had the following children:

a. **Catherine Hire** was married to William Cochran in September 1831.

b. **Althina Hire** was married to a Mr. Decker.

c. **Jane Hire** was married to a Mr. Decker.

d. **Susanah Hire** was married to John Gregory in June 1845.

e. **Mary Hire** was married to Fred Harter on October 31, 1843.

f. **Elizabeth Hire (# 21 on chart)** was born on July 14, 1817. She was married to Josiah Clawson, Sr.

g. **Eliza Jane Hire** was born in 1820.

h. **Martin Hire, Jr.** was born in 1831. He was married to Elizabeth. He died in 1870.

i. **John Hire** was born on March 11, 1834.

40. **Edward Hartshorn, Sr.** was born about 1793 in Delaware or Maryland to George Hartshorn, Sr. and Hannah Oldham. He was married to Lydia DeLong on January 12, 1815 in Washington County, Ohio. He died before 1860 in Bath Twp, Allen County, Ohio.
Edward and Mary Hartshorn bought land in Allen County, Ohio in the 1830's. Mary possibly was a second wife of Edward and the mother of his four younger children. Both Mary and Lydia died before 1850.

41. **Lydia DeLong** was born about 1795 to Jonathan DeLong and Margaret Hamilton. She was married to Edward Hartshorn, Sr. on January 12, 1815 in Washington County, Ohio. She died before 1850.

Edward Hartshorn, Sr. and Lydia DeLong had the following children:

a. **Elmore Hartshorn (# 22 on chart)** was born in 1815. He was married to Casander McHenry.

b. **Elvina Hartshorn** was born in 1821.

c. **Malinda Hartshorn** was born in 1828. She was married to Joseph Satterthwaite on January 1, 1854 in Allen County, Ohio.

d. **Edward Hartshorn, Jr.** was born in 1829. He was married to Elvira. He died in 1874.

e. **Margaret Hartshorn** was born in 1840.

f. **Jethro Hartshorn** was born in 1843.

g. **Lucetta Hartshorn** was born in 1846.

h. **Rosey Hartshorn** was born in 1848.

42. **Isaac McHenry** was born on December 27, 1763 in Hampshire County, Virginia or West Virginia to Samuel McHenry. He was a Baptist Minister. He was married to Margaret Blair in 1795. He was married to Jemima Gaskill on November 20, 1815 in Fayette County, Ohio.

43. **Jemima Gaskill** was born about 1773 in New Jersey to Caleb Gaskill and Hope Rossell. She was married to Isaac McHenry November 20, 1815 in Fayette County, Ohio. She was married to Barnet Evertson. She was a Quaker.

Isaac McHenry and Jemima Gaskill had the following children:

a. **Casander McHenry (# 23 on chart)** was born in 1816. She was married to Elmore Hartshorn.

44. **Johann Heinrich Grothaus** was probably born in Germany. He was married to Catharina Gertrude Lause on October 24, 1786 in Wellingholzhausen, Hanover, Germany and changed his surname to LAUSE. He died and was buried in Germany.

45. **Catharina Gertrude Lause** was born on April 5, 1749 in Wellingholzhausen, Hanover, Germany to Johann Heinrich Lause and Catharina Gertrude Cord. She was married to Johann Grothaus on October 24, 1786 in Wellingholzhausen, Hanover, Germany and she retained her surname LAUSE. She died and was buried in Germany.

Johann Heinrich Grothaus and Catharina Gertrude Lause had the following children:

- a. **David Lause** was born on September 26, 1789 in Wellingholzhausen, Germany.

- b. **Henry Joseph Lause (# 24 on chart)** was born on August 4, 1791. He was married to Mary Elizabeth Giesker.

- c. **Mary Elizabeth Lause** was born on August 24, 1795 in Wellingholzhausen, Germany.

46. **Johannes Andreas Morio** was born to Johannis Petri Morio and Margaretha Voegler. He was married to Anna Maria Leibrecht in Hauenstein, Pfalz, Bayern.

47. **Anna Maria Leibrecht** was born to Nicolai Leibrecht and Margaretha Morio. She was married to Johannes Andreas Morio.

Johannes Andreas Morio and Anna Maria Leibrecht had the following children:

- a. **J. Philippi Morio (# 28 on chart)** was born in 1806. He was married to Margaret Seibel.

48. **Martini Seibel** was married to Elisabethae Cronauer.

49. **Elisabethae Cronauer** was married to Martini Seibel.

Martini Seibel and Elisabethae Cronauer had the following children:

- a. **Margaret Seibel (# 29 on chart)** was born in 1810. She was married to J. Philippi Morio.

SEVENTH GENERATION

50. Leonard Hire was born in 1751 in Pennsylvania or West Virginia to Leonard Heyer and Mary or Anna Maria Hause. He was married to Catherine Rohrbaugh. He later was married to Dolly. Leonard served in the American Revolutionary War. He was a member of the Company of Ensign Stephen Ashby 1775. He died in 1845 in Braxton County, West Virginia.

51. Catherine Rohrbaugh was born to Mr. and Mrs. Adam Rohrbaugh. She was married to Leonard Hire.

Leonard Hire and Catherine Rohrbaugh had the following children:

    a. **Jacob Hire** was married to Mary Homan on August 18, 1805 in Virginia.

    b. **Peter Hire.**

    c. **Christian Hire** was married to Julia or Judy Sirk.

    d. **Mary Hire** was married to Isaac Shaver.

    e. **Leonard Hire** was born in 1782. He was married to Sarah Bush.

    f. **Abraham Hire** was born in 1788 in Virginia. He was married to Uranah Peterson on January 14, 1816 in Green County, Ohio. He died on March 6, 1855 in Van Wert County, Ohio. He was buried in King Cemetery in Middle Point, Ohio.

    g. **Martin Hire (# 38 on chart)** was born in 1792. He was married to Sally (Sarah) Neely.

52. George Hartshorn, Sr. was born between 1745 and 1755. He was married to Hannah Oldham before 1784, possibly in Kent County, Delaware. He died on December 25, 1829 in Jefferson County, Ohio.

A George Hartshorn is listed in the 1800 Delaware census at Grog Town, Duck Creek Hundred, Kent County with 2 males under 10, 1 male 26-45, 1 female under 10, 1 female 16-26. George would have been born between 1755-1774 and his wife would have been born between 1774-1784.

George was in Jefferson County, Ohio in 1820. In his will dated February 21, 1821, he states that he is "old and frail". The will was probated on April 10, 1830. Based on will statement, George was probably born between 1745-1755 and died in Jefferson County, Ohio about 1830.

53. **Hannah Oldham** was born on April 15, 1757 in Chester County, Pennsylvania. She was married to George Hartshorn, Sr. before 1784. She died in 1844 in Coshocton County, Ohio.

George Hartshorn, Sr. and Hannah Oldham had the following children:

a.   **George Hartshorn, Jr.** was born on June 8, 1772 in Kent County, Delaware or Maryland. He possibly was married to Alvira and to Tillith. He died in 1853 in Washington County, Ohio. He was buried in Tower Salem Cemetery.

It is not certain that this George was the husband of Alvira and Tillith and had eight children. It is possible that this George never married and the spouses and children listed belong to a different George Hartshorn. Dr. Nathan Hartshorn, the son of George and Alvira Hartshorn, told his granddaughter the story that grandpap Hartshorn left for the gold rush in California, took sick and died, and was buried in Chillicothe, Missouri. No documentation could be found on this.

b.   **Mary Polly Hartshorn** was born in 1785. She was married to Roland Rogers on November 7, 1805 in Jefferson County, Ohio. She died on October 31, 1840 in Jefferson County, Ohio. She was buried in Cross Creek, Washington County, Pennsylvania.

c.   **Priscilla Inez Hartshorn** was born on November 7, 1788. She was married to David Jones.

    d. **Sprigh E. "Spry" Hartshorn** was born on September 24, 1789. He died on March 24, 1813.

    e. **Hugh Hartshorn** was born about 1791. He was married to Charity Holms.

    f. **Edward Hartshorn, Sr. (# 40 on chart)** was born about 1793. He was married to Lydia DeLong.

    g. **Eliza (Sarah) Hartshorn** was born on February 14, 1793. She was married to James Davis on July 3, 1813 in Marietta, Washington County, Ohio. She died on December 2, 1851 in Caldwell, Noble County, Ohio.

54. **Jonathan DeLong** was born about 1759 in Pennsylvania to Mr. and Mrs. James? DeLong. He was married to Margaret Hamilton. He died on June 26, 1814. He was buried in Salem, Ohio on his Farm.

55. **Margaret Hamilton** was born in Pennsylvania. She was married to Jonathan DeLong.

Jonathan DeLong and Margaret Hamilton had the following children:

    a. **Mary DeLong** was born on August 24, 1785 in Pennsylvania. She was married to Manley Morse in 1805 at Washington County, Ohio. She died on April 10, 1872 in Caldwell, Noble County, Ohio. She was buried in Caldwell, Ohio, Olive Cemetery.

    b. **Isaac Hamilton DeLong** was born in 1789. He was married to Nancy Held or Hill and Nancy or Delcie Lancaster.

    c. **David DeLong** was born about 1790. He was married to Sarah (Sally) Burch.

    d. **Sarah DeLong** was born about 1791. She was married to Thomas C. Gilkerson on April 14, 1809 in Washington County, Ohio.

    e. **Betsy DeLong** was born about 1792. She was married to Joseph Taylor before 1818.

f. **Jonathan DeLong, Jr.** was born in 1794. He was married to Sabina Horn and Harriet.

g. **Lydia DeLong (# 41 on chart)** was born about 1795. She was married to Edward Hartshorn, Sr.

h. **James DeLong** was born in 1796. He was married to Agnes Smith.

i. **Samuel DeLong** was born in 1798. He was married to Jane Fowler.

j. **Chauncey H. DeLong** was born in 1804. He was married to Sarah Grandstaff and Nancy McIntyre. He died on December 4, 1887 in Muskingum County, Ohio.

56. **Samuel McHenry** was born to Mr. and Mrs. Barnaby McHenry. He was married to Unknown Wife. He died in 1810 in Randolph County, Virginia.

Samuel McHenry and his Wife had the following children:

a. **Isaac McHenry (# 42 on chart)** was born on December 27, 1763. He was married to Jemima Gaskill.

57. **Caleb Gaskill** was born about 1741 in Northampton, New Jersey to Josiah Gaskill and Amy Shreve. He was married to Hope Rossell on July 16, 1765. He died in 1817 in Pancoastburg, Ohio.

58. **Hope Rossell** was born in 1747 in Burlington, New Jersey to James Rossell and Elizabeth Allcott. She was married to Caleb Gaskill on July 16, 1765.

Caleb Gaskill and Hope Rossell had the following children:

a. **Jemima Gaskill (# 43 on chart)** was born about 1773. She was married to Isaac McHenry.

59. **Johann Heinrich Lause** was born in Germany. He was married to Catharina Gertrude Cord on October 24, 1746 at

Wellingholzhausen, Hanover, Germany. He died and was buried in Germany.

60. **Catharina Gertrude Cord** was born in Germany. She was married to Johann Heinrich Lause on October 24, 1746 at Wellingholzhausen, Hanover, Germany. She died and was buried in Germany.

Johann Heinrich Lause and Catharina Gertrude Cord had the following children:

- a. **Johann Cord Lause** was born on January 22, 1747 in Germany.

- b. **Catharina Gertrude Lause (# 45 on chart)** was born on April 5, 1749. She was married to Johann Grothaus.

61. **Johannis Petri Morio** was born on May 27, 1747 in Hauenstein, Pfalz, Bayern to Bartholomaeus Morio and Magdalena Scheibin. He was married to Margaretha Voegler in Hauenstein, Pfalz, Bayern. He died in 1806.

62. **Margaretha Voegler** was born to Antony Voegler and Anna Maria Naabin. She was married to Johannis Petri Morio in Hauenstein, Pfalz, Bayern.

Johannis Petri Morio and Margaretha Voegler had the following children:

- a. **Johannes Andreas Morio (# 46 on chart)** was married to Anna Maria Leibrecht.

63. **Nicolai Leibrecht** was married to Margaretha Morio.

64. **Margaretha Morio** was married to Nicolai Leibrecht.

Nicolai Leibrecht and Margaretha Morio had the following children:

- a. **Anna Maria Leibrecht (# 47 on chart)** was married to Johannes Andreas Morio.

EIGHTH GENERATION

65. Leonard Heyer was born on December 25, 1727 in Switzerland to Lienert Heyer and Clara Lutzler. Leonard came to America in 1737 with his parents. He was married to Mary or Anna Maria Hause. He was a Farmer. He died in 1786 in Hardy or Grant County, West Virginia. He was buried in Hardy County, West Virginia.

66. Mary or Anna Maria Hause was born about 1725 in Switzerland to Mr. and Mrs. Peter Hause. She was married to Leonard Heyer. She died in 1790 in Hardy County, West Virginia. She was buried in Hardy County, West Virginia.

Leonard Heyer and Mary or Anna Maria Hause had the following children:

- a. **John Hire** was married to Patience. He died in 1829.

- b. **Lewis Hire** was married to Mariam. He died in 1794 in Hardy or Grant County, West Virginia. He was buried in Hardy or Grant County, West Virginia.

- c. **Peter Hire.**

- d. **Rudolph Hire.**

- e. **Mary Hire** was married to Valentine Powers.

- f. **Leonard Hire (# 50 on chart)** was born in 1751. He was married to Catherine Rohrbaugh.

- g. **Jacob Hire** was born in 1757. He was married to Elizabeth.

- h. **Michael Hire** was born in 1768. He was buried in Hire Graveyard, Ross County, Ohio.

67. Adam Rohrbaugh was married to Unknown Wife.

Adam Rohrbaugh and his Wife had the following children:

- a. **Catherine Rohrbaugh (# 51 on chart)** was married to Leonard Hire.

68. James DeLong (questionable first name) was married to Unknown Wife.

James DeLong and his Wife had the following children:

    a. **Jonathan DeLong (# 54 on chart)** was born about 1759. He was married to Margaret Hamilton.

69. Barnaby McHenry was married to Unknown Wife.

Barnaby McHenry and his Wife had the following children:

    a. **Samuel McHenry (# 56 on chart)** was married to Unknown Wife.

70. Josiah Gaskill was born in 1711 in New Jersey to Josiah Gaskill, Sr. and Rebecca Lippincott. He was married to Amy Shreve on September 7, 1737.

71. Amy Shreve was born about 1719 to Caleb Shreve and Mary Atkinson. She was married to Josiah Gaskill on September 7, 1737.

Josiah Gaskill and Amy Shreve had the following children:

    a. **Caleb Gaskill (# 57 on chart)** was born about 1741. He was married to Hope Rossell.

72. James Rossell was born in 1727 to Zacharia Rossell and Mary Hilliard. He was married to Elizabeth Allcott on May 13, 1745.

73. Elizabeth Allcott was born about 1725. She was married to James Rossell on May 13, 1745.

James Rossell and Elizabeth Allcott had the following children:

    a. **Hope Rossell (# 58 on chart)** was born in 1747. She was married to Caleb Gaskill.

74. **Bartholomaeus Morio** was born in 1710 to Hans Peter Morio and Elizabeth Naab. He was married to Magdalena Scheibin in Hauenstein, Pfalz, Bayern.

75. **Magdalena Scheibin** was married to Bartholomaeus Morio in Hauenstein, Pfalz, Bayern.

Bartholomaeus Morio and Magdalena Scheibin had the following children:

    a. **Johannis Petri Morio (# 61 on chart)** was born on May 27, 1747. He was married to Margaretha Voegler.

76. **Antony Voegler** (questionable spelling of surname) was married to Anna Maria Naabin.

77. **Anna Maria Naabin** was married to Antony Voegler.

Antony Voegler and Anna Maria Naabin had the following children:

    a. **Margaretha Voegler (# 62 on chart)** was married to Johannis Petri Morio.

NINTH GENERATION

78. Lienert Heyer was born in 1696 in Switzerland. Lienert married Clara Lutzler in Switzerland. He had one child from a previous marriage. They came to America (Pennsylvania) in 1737. They moved to West Virginia in 1750. He was a Farmer. He died about 1771 in Hardy County, West Virginia. He was buried in Hardy County, West Virginia.

79. Clara Lutzler was born in 1705 in Switzerland to Rudolph Lutzler. She was married to Lienert Heyer in Switzerland. She died in Hardy County, West Virginia. She was buried in Hardy County, West Virginia.

Lienert Heyer and Clara Lutzler had the following children:

a. **Anna Barbara Heyer** was born on February 22, 1724 in Switzerland. She was married to Jacob Shobe on July 3, 1743 in Tulpehochen, Pennsylvania. She died after 1771 in Hardy County, West Virginia. She was buried in Hardy County, West Virginia.

b. **Elizabeth Heyer** was born on June 17, 1725 in Switzerland. She was married to Martin Shobe in Berks County, Pennsylvania. She died in Grant County, West Virginia. She was buried in Grant County, West Virginia.

c. **Leonard Heyer (# 65 on chart)** was born on December 25, 1727. He was married to Mary or Anna Maria Hause.

d. **Hans Rudolph Heyer** was born on May 29, 1729 in Switzerland. He was married to Nancy. He was an Indian Fighter. He died in 1802 in North Carolina. He was buried in North Carolina.

e. **Hans Ulrich Heyer** was born on July 29, 1731 in Switzerland. He died in 1739 in Pennsylvania as a young child.

f. **Clara Heyer** was born in 1734 in Switzerland. She died in 1737 in England on Journey to America.

g. **Antoni Heyer** was born in 1739. He died young in South Branch of Potomac (now West Virginia).

h. **Magdaline Heyer** was born in 1739 in Tulpehochen, Pennsylvania. She was married to Sigmund Homan and Michael Power, Jr. She died in 1827 in Hardy County, West Virginia.

i. **Eve Heyer** was born in 1742 in Tulpehochen, Pennsylvania. She was married to Sebastian Hagler.

80. **Peter Hause** was married to Unknown Wife.

Peter Hause and his Wife had the following children:

a. **Mary or Anna Maria Hause (# 66 on chart)** was born about 1725. She was married to Leonard Heyer.

81. **Josiah Gaskill, Sr.** was born on September 11, 1678 in Salem, Essex, Massachusetts to Samuel Gaskill and Provided Southwick. He was married to Rebecca Lippincott on April 5, 1704 in Burlington, New Jersey. He died in December 1761 in Northampton Twp, New Jersey.

82. **Rebecca Lippincott** was born on November 24, 1684 in New Jersey to Restore Lippincott and Hannah Shattuck. She was married to Josiah Gaskill, Sr. on April 5, 1704 in Burlington, New Jersey. She died about 1747.

Josiah Gaskill, Sr. and Rebecca Lippincott had the following children:

a. **Josiah Gaskill (# 70 on chart)** was born in 1711. He was married to Amy Shreve.

83. **Caleb Shreve** was born in 1690 in Narumsunk, Burlington, New Jersey to Caleb Shreve, Sr. and Sara Areson. He was married to Mary Atkinson on August 6, 1718 in Burlington, New Jersey. He died in 1746 in Springfield, Burlington, New Jersey.

84. **Mary Atkinson** was born about 1691 in Burlington, New Jersey to William Atkinson and Elizabeth Curtis. She married Caleb Shreve on August 6, 1718 in Burlington, New Jersey.

Caleb Shreve and Mary Atkinson had the following children:

>   a.   **Amy Shreve (# 71 on chart)** was born about 1719. She was married to Josiah Gaskill.

85. **Zacharia Rossell** was born about 1692 in Northampton, Burlington, New Jersey to Thomas Rossell. He was married to Mary Hilliard in 1715 in Northampton, Burlington, New Jersey. He died in 1761.

86. **Mary Hilliard** was born about 1695 in Northampton, Burlington, New Jersey to John Hilliard and Martha Devon. She was married to Zacharia Rossell in 1715 in Northampton, Burlington, New Jersey.

Zacharia Rossell and Mary Hilliard had the following children:

>   a.   **James Rossell (# 72 on chart)** was born in 1727. He was married to Elizabeth Allcott.

87. **William Allcott** was born about 1692 in Burlington, New Jersey. He was married to Ann about 1716 in Burlington, New Jersey.

88. **Ann Allcott** was born about 1696 in Burlington, New Jersey. Ann's maiden name is unknown. She was married to William Allcott about 1716 in Burlington, New Jersey.

William and Ann Allcott had the following children:

>   a.   **Elizabeth Allcott (# 73 on chart)** was born about 1725. She was married to James Rossell.

89. **Hans Peter Morio** was born in 1675. He was married to Elizabeth Naab. He died in 1748.

90. **Elizabeth Naab** was married to Hans Peter Morio.

Hans Peter Morio and Elizabeth Naab had the following children:

>   a.   **Bartholomaeus Morio (# 74 on chart)** was born in 1710. He was married to Magdalena Scheibin.

TENTH GENERATION

91. **Rudolph Lutzler** was born in 1677. He was married to Unknown Wife.

Rudolph Lutzler and his Wife had the following children:

    a. **Clara Lutzler (# 79 on chart)** was born in 1705. She was married to Lienert Heyer.

92. **Samuel Gaskill** was born on August 7, 1639 in Salem, Essex, Massachusetts to Edward and Sarah Gaskill. He was married to Provided Southwick on October 30, 1662 in Salem, Essex, Massachusetts. He died about 1723.

93. **Provided Southwick** was born on December 6, 1641 in Salem, Essex, Massachusetts to Lawrence and Cassandra Southwick. She was married to Samuel Gaskill on October 30, 1662 in Salem, Essex, Massachusetts. She died on April 12, 1727.

Samuel Gaskill and Provided Southwick had the following children:

    a. **Josiah Gaskill, Sr. (# 81 on chart)** was born on September 11, 1678. He was married to Rebecca Lippincott.

94. **Restore Lippincott** was born on July 3, 1653 in Plymouth, Devonshire, England to Richard Lippincott and Abigail Goody. He was married to Hannah Shattuck on November 6, 1674 in Shrewsbury, Monmouth, New Jersey. He died on July 10, 1741 in Mt. Holly, Burlington, New Jersey.

95. **Hannah Shattuck** was born on July 8, 1654 in Boston, Suffolk, Massachusetts to William and Hannah Shattuck. She was married to Restore Lippincott on November 6, 1674 in Shrewsbury, Monmouth, New Jersey. She died in 1729.

Restore Lippincott and Hannah Shattuck had the following children:

> a. **Rebecca Lippincott (# 82 on chart)** was born on November 24, 1684. She was married to Josiah Gaskill, Sr.

96. **Caleb Shreve, Sr.** was born in 1652 in Portsmouth, Newport, Rhode Island to Thomas and Martha Shreve. He was married to Sara Areson in 1680 in Fort Monmouth, Burlington, New Jersey. He died in 1741 in New Jersey.

97. **Sara Areson** was born about 1657 in Long Island, New York. She was married to Caleb Shreve, Sr. in 1680 in Fort Monmouth, Burlington, New Jersey. She died in Burlington, New Jersey.

Caleb Shreve, Sr. and Sara Areson had the following children:

> a. **Caleb Shreve (# 83 on chart)** was born in 1690. He was married to Mary Atkinson.

98. **William Atkinson** was born about 1661 in England. He died in 1714 in Burlington, New Jersey. He was married to Elizabeth Curtis on March 9, 1686 in Burlington, New Jersey.

99. **Elizabeth Curtis** was born on May 21, 1666 in England to Thomas and Jane Curtis. She was married to William Atkinson on March 9, 1686 in Burlington, New Jersey. She died in 1714 in Springfield, Burlington, New Jersey.

William Atkinson and Elizabeth Curtis had the following children:

> a. **Mary Atkinson (# 84 on chart)** was born about 1691. She was married to Caleb Shreve.

100. **Thomas Rossell** was born about 1669 in Newton, Long Island, New York to Major John Rossell and Mary Johnson. He was married to Unknown Wife.

101. **Mrs. Thomas Rossell** was born about 1670. She was married to Thomas Rossell.

Mr. and Mrs. Thomas Rossell had the following children:

    a. **Zacharia Rossell (# 85 on chart)** was born about 1692. He was married to Mary Hilliard.

102. **John Hilliard** was born in Northampton, Burlington, New Jersey. He was married to Martha Devon.

103. **Martha Devon** was born in Northampton, Burlington, New Jersey.

John Hilliard and Martha Devon had the following children:

    a. **Mary Hilliard (# 86 on chart)** was born about 1695. She was married to Zacharia Rossell.

ELEVENTH GENERATION

104. Edward Gaskill was born about 1603 in Salem, Essex, Massachusetts. He was married to Sarah about 1638 in Salem, Essex, Massachusetts. He died about 1690.

105. Sarah Gaskill was born about 1617 in Salem, Essex, Massachusetts. Sarah's maiden name is unknown. She was married to Edward Gaskill about 1638 in Salem, Essex, Massachusetts.

Edward and Sarah Gaskill had the following children:

> a. **Samuel Gaskill (# 92 on chart)** was born on August 7, 1639. He was married to Provided Southwick.

106. Lawrence Southwick was born about 1613. He was married to Cassandra in Massachusetts. He died in 1660 in Shelter Island, Suffolk, New York.

107. Cassandra Southwick was married to Lawrence Southwick in Massachusetts. Cassandra's maiden name is unknown. She died in 1660 in Shelter Island, Suffolk, New York.

Lawrence and Cassandra Southwick had the following children:

> a. **Provided Southwick (# 93 on chart)** was born on December 6, 1641. She was married to Samuel Gaskill.

108. Richard Lippincott was born about 1615 in Devonshire, England to Anthony Lippincott and Margery Weere. He was married to Abigail Goody on May 10, 1640 in Roxbury, Suffolk, Massachusetts. Richard and his wife, Abigail, immigrated to America about 1640. In 1652 they returned to England. About 1661, Richard and his family returned to America. Richard died on November 25, 1683 in Shrewsbury, Monmouth, New Jersey.

109. Abigail Goody was born about 1620 in Northumberland, England. She was married to Richard Lippincott on May 10, 1640 in

Roxbury, Suffolk, Massachusetts. She died on July 2, 1697 in Shrewsbury, Monmouth, New Jersey.

Richard Lippincott and Abigail Goody had the following children:

- a. **Remembrance Lippincott** was born in July 1641 in Dorchester, Massachusetts.

- b. **John Lippincott** was born on November 6, 1644 in Boston, Suffolk, Massachusetts. He died on April 16, 1720 in Shrewsbury, Monmouth, New Jersey.

- c. **Abigail Lippincott** was born on January 17, 1646 in Boston, Suffolk, Massachusetts. She died in 1646 in Boston, Suffolk, Massachusetts.

- d. **Restore Lippincott (# 94 on chart)** was born on July 3, 1653. He was married to Hannah Shattuck.

- e. **Freedom Lippincott** was born in 1655 in Plymouth, Devonshire, England.

- f. **Increase Lippincott** was born in 1657 in Plymouth, Devonshire, England. She was married to Samuel Dennis.

- g. **Jacob Lippincott** was born in 1660 in Plymouth, Devonshire, England.

- h. **Preserve Lippincott** was born on December 25, 1663 in America.

110. **William Shattuck** was born about 1628 in Boston, Suffolk, Massachusetts. He was married to Hannah about 1653 in Boston, Suffolk, Massachusetts. He died about 1693 in Monmouth, New Jersey.

111. **Hannah Shattuck** was born about 1630. Hannah's maiden name is unknown. She was married to William Shattuck about 1653 in Boston, Suffolk, Massachusetts.

William and Hannah Shattuck had the following children:

- a. **Hannah Shattuck (# 95 on chart)** was born on July 8, 1654. She was married to Restore Lippincott.

112. **Thomas Shreve** was born in 1623 in Portsmouth, Newport, Rhode Island to William and Oara Shreve. He was married to Martha about 1647 in Rhode Island. He died on May 29, 1675.

113. **Martha Shreve** was born about 1627 in Newport, Rhode Island. Martha's maiden name is unknown. She was married to Thomas Shreve about 1647 in Rhode Island. She died in 1691.

Thomas and Martha Shreve had the following children:

    a. **Caleb Shreve, Sr. (# 96 on chart)** was born in 1652. He was married to Sara Areson.

114. **Thomas Curtis** was born in Burgbrook, England. He was married to Jane about 1660 in Burgbrook, England. He died in 1688 in Burlington, New Jersey.

115. **Jane Curtis** was born about 1639 in England. Jane's maiden name is unknown. She was married to Thomas Curtis about 1660 in Burgbrook, England.

Thomas and Jane Curtis had the following children:

    a. **Elizabeth Curtis (# 99 on chart)** was born on May 21, 1666. She was married to William Atkinson.

116. **Major John Rossell** was born about 1633 in England to Mr. and Mrs. John Rossell. He was married to Mary Johnson in 1668 in London, England.

117. **Mary Johnson** was born about 1635 in England. She was married to Major John Rossell in 1668 in London, England.

Major John Rossell and Mary Johnson had the following children:

    a. **Thomas Rossell (# 100 on chart)** was born about 1669. He was married to Unknown Wife.

TWELFTH GENERATION

118. **Anthony Lippincott** was born on November 4, 1593 in Sydbury, Devon, England to Bartholomew and Alice Lippincott. He was married to Margery Weere about 1615 in England. He died on January 8, 1619.

119. **Margery Weere** was born about 1595 in Tregony, Cornwall, England. She was married to Anthony Lippincott about 1615 in England.

Anthony Lippincott and Margery Weere had the following children:

    a. **Richard Lippincott (# 108 on chart)** was born about 1615. He was married to Abigail Goody.

120. **William Shreve** was born about 1592 in Isle of Wight, H, England to Sir William Shreve and Lady Jane Fairfax. He was married to Oara. He died in Portsmouth, Newport, Rhode Island.

121. **Oara Shreve** was born about 1594 in Amsterdam, Netherlands. Oara's maiden name is unknown. She was married to William Shreve. She died in Portsmouth, Newport, Rhode Island.

William and Oara Shreve had the following children:

    a. **Thomas Shreve (# 112 on chart)** was born in 1623. He was married to Martha.

122. **John Rossell** was born, died and buried in England. He was married to Unknown Wife in 1630 in England.

123. **Mrs. John Rossell** was born in 1610 in England. Her name is unknown. She was married to John Rossell in 1630 in England.

Mr. and Mrs. John Rossell had the following children:

    a. **Major John Rossell (# 116 on chart)** was born about 1633. He was married to Mary Johnson.

THIRTEENTH GENERATION

124. Bartholomew Lippincott was born about 1567 in Sydbury, Devon, England to Anthony Lippincott, Sr. and Katharine Orrels. He was married to Alice about 1592 in Sydbury, Devon, England.

125. Alice Lippincott was born about 1571 in Sydbury, Devon, England. Alice's maiden name is unknown. She was married to Bartholomew Lippincott about 1592 in Sydbury, Devon, England.

Bartholomew and Alice Lippincott had the following children:

    a. Anthony Lippincott (# 118 on chart) was born on November 4, 1593. He was married to Margery Weere.

126. Sir William Shreve was married to Lady Jane Fairfax.

127. Lady Jane Fairfax was married to Sir William Shreve.

Sir William Shreve and Lady Jane Fairfax had the following children:

    a. William Shreve (# 120 on chart) was born about 1592. He was married to Oara.

FOURTEENTH GENERATION

128. **Anthony Lippincott, Sr.** was born about 1540 in Eastwood, Devonshire, England to John Lippincott, Sr. and Anne Elforde. He was married to Katharine Orrels about 1561 in Devonshire, England.

129. **Katharine Orrels** was born about 1543 in Devonshire, England. She was married to Anthony Lippincott, Sr. about 1561 in Devonshire, England.

Anthony Lippincott, Sr. and Katharine Orrels had the following children:

    a. **Bartholomew Lippincott (# 124 on chart)** was born about 1567. He was married to Alice.

FIFTEENTH GENERATION

130. **John Lippincott, Sr.** was born about 1513 in England. He was married to Anne Elforde about 1535 in Devonshire, England.

131. **Anne Elforde** was born about 1515 in Kilkampton, Cornwall, England. She was married to John Lippincott, Sr. about 1535 in Devonshire, England.

John Lippincott, Sr. and Anne Elforde had the following children:

    a. **Anthony Lippincott, Sr. (# 128 on chart)** was born about 1540. He was married to Katharine Orrels.

Index

Please note that numbers in *italics* refer to the Pedigree Chart, in **bold** refer to photos included in the main text, and those in plain font refer to the main text.

About the Author

Born, reared and educated in the Midwest, the author always felt a strong pull to the West and its native peoples. Perhaps this curiosity came from the Indian name given to her by her father or her family's stories about the Indians who had once lived on the land claimed by her ancestors. Whatever the reasons, Winona Garmhausen moved to the Southwest in 1972 and devoted the next twenty-seven years to working with and for native American peoples.

Her Southwestern Indian friends nudged her toward seeking out the Native Americans whose memories and artifacts she had grown up with in the northwest corner of Ohio. During this personal journey, Winona found her ancestors and the Shawnee Indians who had lived side by side as neighbors and friends.

Winona Garmhausen holds a Ph.D. in American Studies from The University of New Mexico.